Professional Development for Teachers

Teaching and Assessing Skills in
Geography

Steve Sibley

CAMBRIDGE
UNIVERSITY PRESS

CAMBRIDGE UNIVERSITY PRESS
Cambridge, New York, Melbourne, Madrid, Cape Town,
Singapore, São Paulo, Delhi, Tokyo, Mexico City

Cambridge University Press
The Edinburgh Building, Cambridge CB2 8RU, UK

Published in the United States of America by
Cambridge University Press, New York

www.cambridge.org
Information on this title: www.cambridge.org/9780521682992

First published 2008
Third printing 2010

A catalogue record for this publication is available from the British Library

Library of Congress Cataloguing in Publication Data

Downing, Lisa.
  The Cambridge introduction to Michel Foucault / Lisa Downing.
    p.   cm.
  Includes bibliographical references and index.
  ISBN 978-0-521-86443-5 (hardback)
  1. Foucault, Michel, 1926–1984.   I. Title.
  B2430.F724D69 2008
  194 – dc22   2008020089

ISBN 978-0-521-86443-5 Hardback
ISBN 978-0-521-68299-2 Paperback

Contents

Foreword

Teaching is a complex and demanding profession. All over the world, societies change in response to new knowledge gained, technological developments, globalisation and a requirement for an ever-more sophisticated and educated population. Teachers are in the forefront of such social change, responding with speed and confidence to the new demands made of them, in terms of both their knowledge and the way in which they teach. This series is intended to help them in their adaptation to change and in their professional development as teachers.

Curriculum changes worldwide are putting increased emphasis on the acquisition of skills as well as subject knowledge, so that students will have the ability to respond flexibly to the swiftly changing modern environment. As a result, teachers must be able both to teach and assess skills and to adjust their own teaching methods to embrace a wider range of techniques for both teaching and assessing in the classroom. The books in this series are practical handbooks which explore these techniques and offer advice on how to use them to enhance the teacher's own practice.

The handbooks are written by teachers with direct experience of teaching and assessing skills at this level. We have asked them to write for their readers in such a way that the readers feel directly supported in their professional development. Thus, as well as tasks for students, there are tasks for teachers, pauses for reflection and questions to be answered. We hope that readers will find that this mixture of the practical and the professional helps them, both in their practice and in their own sense of what it means to be an effective teacher in this modern, changing world of international education.

Dr Kate Pretty
Series Editor

1 Introduction

Purpose and contents

This book is aimed at teachers throughout the world involved in teaching Geography and related subjects at IGCSE, O Level and similar levels who are seeking to enhance their professional expertise in the classroom. Many Geography teachers in international schools are, to a large extent, working on their own, as frequently there may only be one Geography teacher on the staff and the nearest neighbour may be hundreds of kilometres away. Also, not all Geography teachers are subject specialists. They may be historians, economists or scientists, expected to teach a range of subjects to examination level. Whatever your situation, this book will provide advice and a range of ideas. You can use them straight away or adapt them to fit your syllabus or location needs. While many of the examples given are directly linked to the IGCSE syllabuses in Geography, Development Studies and Environmental Management, the ideas can be used with any examination syllabus and with students of any age.

In particular, I shall focus on strategies which you can use, not only to improve examination skills and performance, but also to encourage stimulating classroom approaches, enabling students of all abilities to achieve their full potential. Wherever possible, I have illustrated theoretical references to the teaching and assessment of skills in Geography with examples of lessons which I have taught or seen working successfully.

What use is Geography?

As people in all parts of the world become increasingly interdependent, Geography helps to give people a knowledge and understanding of life at a local, regional and global level. An appreciation of different cultures is important to make the most of life in a multicultural society. Furthermore, in a world where there is much concern over threats to the environment, Geography tackles the big issue of environmental responsibility.

Effective teaching and learning in Geography require a clear understanding of the purpose of the subject and how it is able to make distinctive contributions to the school curriculum (see Figure 1).

In the UK, it is the view of the Geographical Association (1999) that the aims of a geographical education are:

- to develop in young people a **knowledge and understanding** of:
  - where they live, other people and places, and how people and places interrelate and interconnect;
  - the significance of location;
  - human and physical environments;
  - people–environment relationships;
  - the causes and consequences of change;
- to develop the **skills** needed to carry out geographical study (e.g. geographical enquiry, mapwork and fieldwork);
- to stimulate an **interest** in, and to encourage an appreciation of, the world around us;
- to develop an **informed concern for the world** around us, and an ability and willingness to take action both locally and globally.

Teacher activity 1.1

- Which of the contributions do you consider to be most significant?

- Review your teaching programme for each class to assess whether enough opportunities are being provided to make the most of each of the distinctive contributions of Geography.

You may find it useful to produce a matrix for each of your classes to help you to assess whether your teaching of Geography is contributing fully or whether there are any aspects shown in Figure 1 which need to be included more frequently.

Key elements of effective teaching and learning in Geography

From the planning stage through to the final preparation of candidates for external examinations, there are many things you can do to make learning effective in the Geography classroom. These can be summarised by the following

- planning teaching content;
- implementing teaching strategies;
- assessment;
- preparation for external examinations.

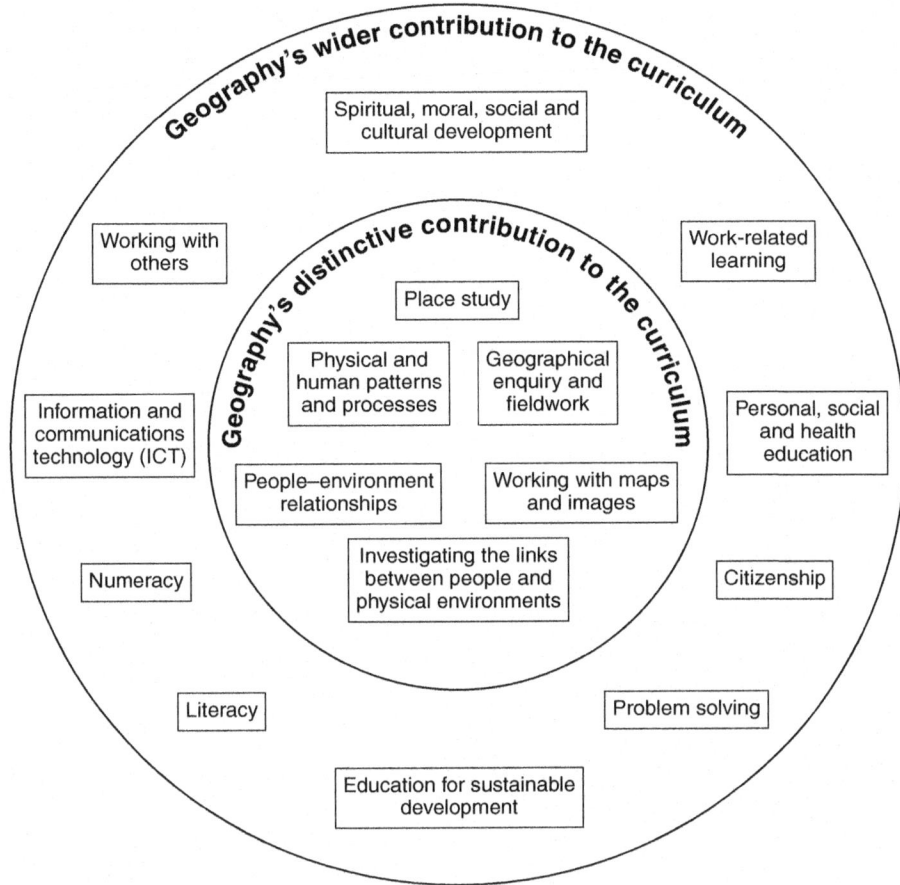

Figure 1: Geography's contribution to the curriculum (Source: Carter 1999)

Planning teaching content

Whether your teaching is structured using a systematic framework (e.g. physical, human and environmental themes), or built around a spatial framework, you should carefully work out your teaching programme in advance to make sure that examination syllabuses are covered in full and appropriate links made to the wider curriculum. Examples which you select for study should be at various scales (local, regional, national and global). There should be an appropriate balance between countries at different levels of economic development. This is known as the context.

You should try to achieve continuity by building on knowledge, understanding and skills, so that students can make successful transitions between different stages of their education and through the course you have planned.

Chapter 2 looks at how to convert an examination syllabus into a teaching programme, giving illustrations of how to use case studies from the local area and further afield. Chapter 6 provides advice on how to incorporate coursework and fieldwork activities into teaching programmes.

Implementing teaching strategies

The success of your teaching will largely depend on how effective you are in using a variety of teaching strategies to make Geography interesting and accessible to all students. You will need to take into account ability, gender and ethnicity.

While a didactic approach, which involves students listening and writing, may be appropriate in some situations and for some students, there are many other strategies which can be used to provide variety. As a Geography teacher, it is not hard to make lessons interesting: not only is the content varied and relevant, but also activities in lessons can range from the didactic to much more active approaches such as individual and group investigations (involving both fieldwork and secondary research), problem solving, resource-based learning, discussions and simulations.

Teaching and learning objectives need to be clear and appropriate. If you share them with students they will be in a better position to understand what they are expected to do and why. Returning to them frequently allows students to check their understanding and make their own judgements about their progress.

Chapter 3 identifies the ways in which you can teach Geography to students of varying abilities. It looks at teaching and learning strategies which you can use with mixed ability classes and sets of both low and high ability students. Chapter 4 investigates a number of different teaching approaches and learning activities, illustrating these with examples. Chapter 5 considers selection of geographical resources and describes, with examples, how some can be used.

Assessment

You should assess work regularly in order to provide feedback to students, to make secure judgements and predictions and to inform future planning of teaching and learning activities. Regular assessments will make students aware of their strengths and weaknesses, enabling them to identify what they need to do to improve. They will also help you to plan appropriate future tasks which focus on both individual and class needs.

You should incorporate a variety of assessment tasks to enable your students to show their knowledge, understanding and skills in different ways. Sharing mark schemes with students enables them to assess their own work against external standards. Furthermore, offering them frequent opportunities for self-assessment allows them to set targets for themselves.

Chapter 7 advises on how you can assess work assignments of different types.

Preparation for external examinations

The extent to which candidates succeed in an external examination will depend on a variety of factors. You can, however, do a great deal in the period leading up to the examinations, in order to prepare them to use their knowledge, understanding and skills to maximum effect. Chapter 7 considers the structure and demands of examination questions and their mark schemes. It provides advice on how to guide candidates in responding to command words used by examiners and gives practical guidance for examination success. It identifies and exemplifies revision strategies which can be of benefit to individuals or for you to use with the whole class.

 LOOKING BACK

Take time now to reflect on the importance and relevance of the subject which you are teaching. Look again at Figure 1 to remind yourself of the contribution which your teaching can make to the curriculum. Ask yourself whether you are taking every opportunity which presents itself:

- Do you study a variety of real places with your students and do you provide regular opportunities for geographical enquiry and fieldwork?
- Do you encourage and facilitate the use of information and communications technology (ICT)?
- Do you think carefully about the development of both literacy and numeracy, and also involve students in collaborative work and problem solving?
- Do you take every opportunity which arises to maximise the potential of Geography to contribute to social and cultural development and educate students for sustainable development?
- Above all, do you want your students to become independent learners and enjoy Geography?

2 Planning teaching content

The importance of planning

The well-prepared Geography teacher will want to ensure that all details of courses taught are worked out well in advance. You will want to ensure that you provide a well-balanced programme of study for each of your classes, identifying opportunities for students to benefit from each of the distinctive contributions of Geography. For classes starting external courses, you need to prepare schemes of work which ensure that the syllabuses are covered in full so students are adequately prepared for all assessed components. You may find it useful to consult both colleagues within your school and other local teachers, in order to draw on each others' experiences in developing work programmes.

This chapter considers how a syllabus produced by an external awarding body, such as Cambridge International Examinations (CIE), should be used to guide the planning of a detailed programme of study. It looks at how the aims and assessment objectives, as well as the content statements, should be used when devising units of work. It also considers how to incorporate appropriate case studies.

The examples referred to here are from the CIE IGCSE syllabuses for Geography and Development Studies. However, you can use any syllabus for the suggested tasks.

The structure of a syllabus

A syllabus produced by an awarding body is a document which outlines in detail those aspects which need to be incorporated by teachers who enter candidates for assessment in that subject. It is a vital document, used not only by teachers to plan the details of the content and structure of their own courses, but also by examiners when producing examination papers.

The important components of a syllabus include:

- The **aims** of the syllabus, comprising both the educational purposes of the course, which may be assessed in examinations, and general outcomes.

- The **assessment objectives**, comprising the sets of skills and activities which are assessed and enable candidates to demonstrate achievement – they may be interrelated or independent.
- An outline of the **assessment structure**, describing the methods which will be used to assess what candidates know, understand and can do. It will include information on the format and length of each examination component, along with details of any coursework requirements. For each component, details will be provided of its weighting as a part of the entire assessment, along with the weighting of the assessment objectives which will be tested by it.
- Details of the required **curriculum content**, identifying the nature of the subject material to be studied. It guides the teacher in selecting appropriate material and case studies to illustrate either a number of major themes or a series of key concepts and questions. It may also specify the scale and context of study for each topic or case study.

Teacher activity 2.1

This exercise uses the syllabus for the CIE IGCSE Development Studies. However, you may choose to do the exercise using another external examination syllabus.

Use the details from either CIE IGCSE Development Studies (given on page 8) or any other syllabus to make sure that you understand the distinctive features of the aims, assessment objectives and assessment structure used:

- Write them out as a brief summary, imagining that you are explaining them to a new teacher at your school.
- Try to identify which of the aims are assessed by the assessment objectives (and where and how they are assessed) and which are more general learning outcomes.

Converting the syllabus into a programme of study

Once you have internalised the aims and assessment objectives of a syllabus, it is time for you to plan a programme of study. This should ensure that the appropriate content is delivered, while at the same time giving students enough opportunities to develop their competence in all the required assessment objectives. In drawing up your programme, it is also crucial to maintain an appropriate balance between countries at

Aims	Assessment objectives	Assessment Structure
• To analyse development as a concept and in practice within the socio-economic, political and resource contexts of a given society • To understand development terminology and elementary development theory • To acquire the skills of analysis necessary to understand the interrelationships of socio-economic, political and resource systems • To critically examine and evaluate different development strategies and experiences • To understand both the prospects for and constraints upon development • To understand the interrelationships of development at local, national, regional and international levels • To appreciate their own actual and potential talents and the resource potential of their environment, so as to utilise these fully for the development of their societies • To participate meaningfully in community efforts to counter poverty, exploitation and other forms of injustice • To develop a challenging attitude so they can act upon their environment to change it in the best interests of everyone	• Knowledge with understanding • Analysis and evaluation • Investigation • Participation and problem solving	• Paper 1: consists of questions involving primarily the demonstration of knowledge and understanding • Paper 2: consists of two structured questions based upon several pieces of related source material, involving primarily the analysis and evaluation of evidence Either • Paper 3 (Coursework): consists of the use of research techniques and a variety of sources in conducting an investigation into a development problem, proposing solutions and carrying out practical activities related to these solutions Or • Paper 4 (Alternative to coursework): candidates provided with a limited amount of data about a development problem which could provide the basis for a project. They will be required to identify questions raised by the data and to indicate ways in which a project could be organised in order to identify and implement solutions

Source: CIE IGCSE Development Studies (2002)

different levels of economic development and at varied scales. Your syllabus may provide some guidance in choosing case studies. However, if this is not the case, it is wise to spread your examples across a variety of geographical areas, using local, regional and national examples where appropriate. Students can often learn best from examples which are most familiar to them, so it is helpful to use local case studies wherever possible.

In drawing up your programme of study, I would suggest the use of a matrix style which provides key information such as this:

Possible activities or case studies	Number of lessons/ timing	Assessment objectives	Context	Scale	Suggested resources

If you produce a matrix for each theme of the syllabus, this will help to ensure that your coverage is thorough. While many teachers develop programmes of study which clearly separate each theme to be taught, there are often opportunities to integrate different parts of the syllabus. This could be beneficial to you as you may then be able to plan your teaching time more effectively. Students may also benefit by being encouraged to appreciate the interaction which takes place between geographical phenomena.

Suggested approaches to planning a unit of work on leisure activities and tourism

This example is based on theme 3 of the CIE IGCSE Geography syllabus on 'Economic development and the use of resources'. The relevant curriculum content for leisure activities and tourism is as follows:
- describe and account for the growth of leisure facilities and tourism in relation to the main attractions of the physical and human landscapes;
- assess the benefits and disadvantages of tourism to a receiving area.

The assessment objectives in CIE IGCSE Geography are:
- knowledge with understanding;
- analysis;
- judgement and decision making;
- investigation.

It would be useful for you to set the scene by defining leisure activities and using statistics to describe and account for the growth of the leisure and tourist industry in a global context.

It may then be possible to use cartographic resources showing the relative popularity of various countries in a region (or areas within a country) to tourists. This would establish the link between tourist numbers and the attractions of the physical and human environment. Atlases could be used to extract information about important physical factors such as climate, enabling students to look for links between these and tourist numbers. At this stage, case studies of important tourist destinations would be appropriate. It may also be possible for you to involve students in investigative tasks. For example, they could find out about the attractions of contrasting destinations, using readily available and up-to-date materials such as tourist brochures and websites. This could be done individually or in groups, and it could lead to display work or oral presentations.

The benefits and disadvantages of tourism to receiving areas should then be considered, again by reference to case study materials. It may be possible to refer to the same case studies as previously used, although there may be advantages in using different case studies in order to vary context and scale. For example, if you used a coastal resort on the Mediterranean island of Majorca to illustrate the main attractions to tourists, then perhaps it would be useful to look at the impacts of tourism on a country such as Kenya. This would provide a change of focus from local to national, developed to developing country and European to African destination.

Whatever the chosen case study, there are, of course, many interesting activities in which students could be involved. Whether through the use of video materials or written text, they will need to be made aware of positive and negative impacts of tourism on people and the environment in the chosen area. It may be possible for you to introduce an element of role play here, involving students in a simulation where they are required to empathise with individuals or interest groups who would be affected by the expansion of tourism in the study area.

This topic is an ideal one to use to encourage an appreciation of the natural environment amongst students and to show how people and the environment are interdependent. It would be an opportunity to consider sustainability by involving students in making recommendations about the future of tourist development in the chosen areas.

Use some of the ideas suggested, together with any ideas of your own, to produce a matrix which plans a unit of work on 'Leisure activities and tourism' for CIE IGCSE Geography. Try to make sure that you include a variety of interesting activities, using resources and case studies at a variety of scales and contexts.

Alternatively, you could produce a matrix on any unit of work for a syllabus of your choice.

The use of case study materials

The case study approach is now commonly used with most age groups. A case study is not an end in itself, but a vehicle for achieving understanding and ensuring that ideas can be illustrated by using real places. Case studies are used to exemplify an issue or theme, and to illustrate generality rather than uniqueness. Through case studies, it is possible to bring alive issues which may be conceptual, in order to increase interest, motivation and understanding.

Resource materials are readily available for many case studies and you can make sure they are topical and up to date by using newspapers, magazines and websites. Many examination syllabuses require case study knowledge to be shown by candidates and students need to be taught in such a way that they can:

- select and recall the relevant points about their case studies;
- recall details which make the case study place specific, rather than simply adding a name to a series of general points;
- show understanding of the generalisations which the case study illustrates;
- select appropriate case studies to respond to examination requirements.

In order to achieve this, you could:

- use case studies to focus clearly on relevant key ideas and skills within the syllabus;
- identify opportunities to use varied resource materials in case studies;
- identify geographical skills which can be developed by using resource materials;
- develop opportunities for differentiation through the resource materials used and a variety of tasks;
- develop case studies to facilitate coursework;
- develop generalisations from case study specifics;
- use a range of examples from different locations, scales and contexts;

- identify ways in which case studies are interrelated at a variety of scales;
- ensure that place-specific details are available to students, to establish an appreciation of the distinctiveness of places.

Suggested approaches to teaching case studies about flooding

The following are examples of case studies of flooding which illustrate a variety of context, scale and location. They also give some examples of learning activities which you could use and skills which could be developed by using them. The suggestions are not exhaustive and could, of course, be applied to other similar examples.

Student activity 2.1

Case study: River Trent
Context: More economically developed country (MEDC)
Scale: Local
Location: UK

The River Trent floods its flood plain regularly in the area shown in Figure 2, although it is now controlled to some extent as shown in Figure 3. You could use the photograph and map to identify the potential effects of flooding and the obvious need for management. The resources give an ideal opportunity to reinforce terms such as 'meander' and 'flood plain', as these features can easily be identified. Learning activities could include photograph and map interpretation, with outline maps or sketches of the area being annotated by students to indicate the disruption that flooding may cause for people in the area.

Figure 2: Flooding of the River Trent

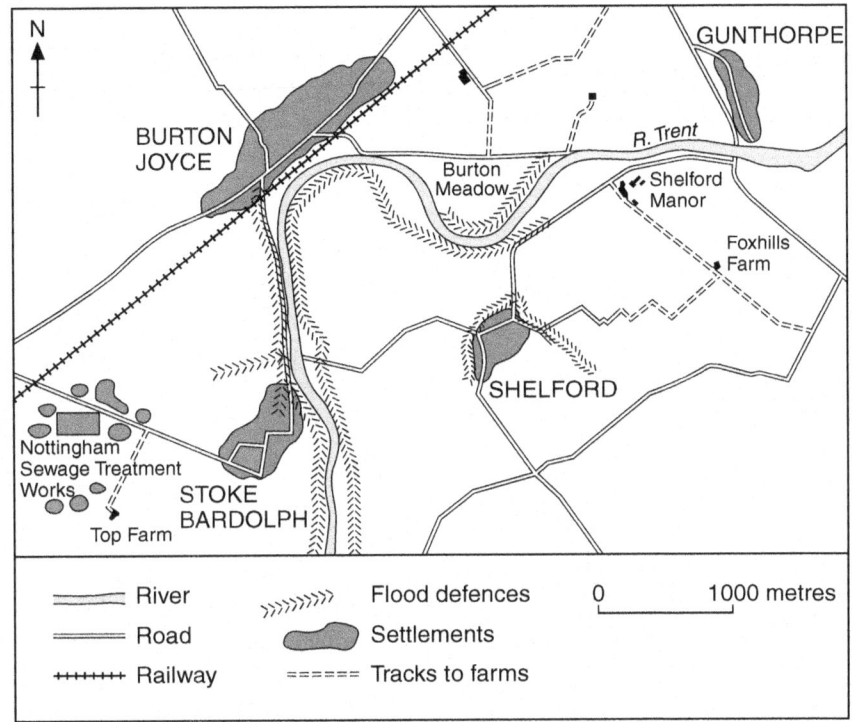

Figure 3: Map of part of the flood plain of the River Trent (Source: OCR Geography A 1586/01 May/June 2002)

Previous attempts to control flooding can be identified from the map and there is the possibility of discussion or role play about the need for further protective measures. Some students could take on roles such as local farmers and residents of villages such as Burton Joyce, while others could take the roles of local councillors and flood protection experts. Discussion could follow on the costs and benefits of flood protection and the impact of possible engineering schemes on the natural environment.

Student activity 2.2

Case study: River Rhine
Context: MEDC
Scale: Regional
Location: Europe

Flooding of the River Rhine, particularly in lowland parts of Germany and the Netherlands, may occur after periods of heavy rainfall. In spring this is often particularly severe, with increases in temperatures in its gathering grounds in the Alps melting large amounts of snow and ice. The case study is ideal to use to illustrate the climatic causes of floods. It is possible to design learning activities which incorporate the analysis of hydrographs (Figure 4) and the use of resource material in atlases.

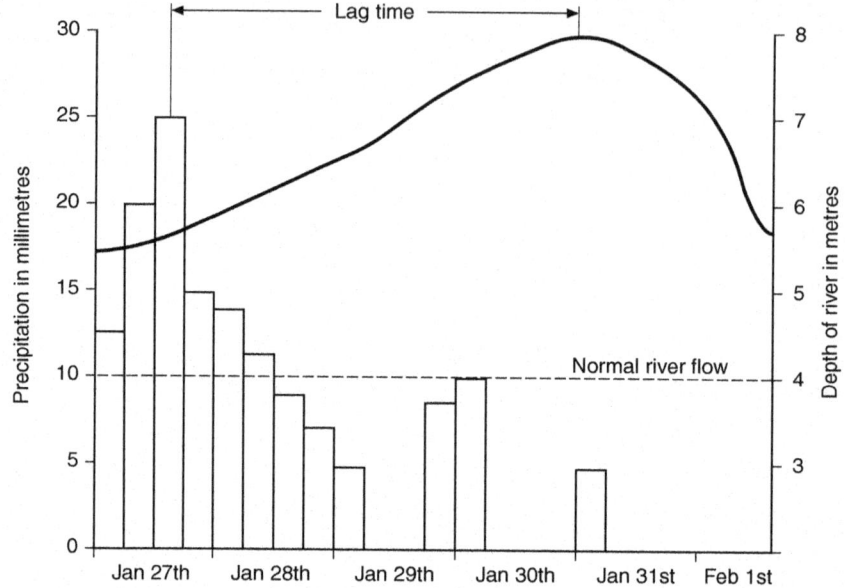

Figure 4: Hydrograph of the River Rhine near Cologne

A starting point could be the drawing and interpretation of a map showing the course of the Rhine. You could ask students to use skills such as the use of the scale to measure the river's length and the interpretation of the key to identify the height of the land around it in various places. You could then use the hydrograph to illustrate the impact of heavy rain on the river and explain the reasons for the time lag. Extension work could involve the use of climatic data in order to identify periods when melting snow in Alpine areas is likely to be a threat.

Student activity 2.3

Case study: The floods in Mozambique in 2000
Context: Less economically developed country (LEDC)
Scale: National
Location: Africa

It is not hard to capture the interest of students when using topical information and unfortunately flood events are all too regular. Their impacts are often devastating in developing countries, where flood plains are densely populated and measures to protect people from flooding are largely non-existent.

The disadvantage of choosing to use current events is that you will never find them in textbooks. This need not be a problem as there is extensive information in newspapers, on the television and radio, and on the Internet. A good search engine – such as www.google.com – can be used to find websites on current events.

Using up-to-date examples in this way provides an ideal opportunity for research, whether individually, in pairs or in groups. Both the causes and effects could be investigated and feedback could be in the form of written reports or presentations.

Teacher activity 2.3

Use a world map to plot the location of the case studies which you teach. This will enable you to see whether your examples are taken from a wide enough range of locations or whether there are any parts of the world which are not properly represented.

Use colour coding on your map or symbols to indicate the scale and context of your case studies in order to help you assess whether the balance is appropriate.

 ## LOOKING BACK

This chapter has emphasised the need for a diligent approach to planning in order to make the most of all opportunities. It makes little difference whether you are considering an individual lesson or the delivery of an entire syllabus. If it has been carefully thought out, it is much more likely to be successful.

Look back at some of the issues covered in this chapter and ask yourself:

- Do I need to take another look at how I organise my teaching?
- Should I reorganise the way in which I teach examination syllabuses?
- Am I making the most of opportunities to plan as a team with colleagues in my school?
- How could I benefit from working more closely and sharing ideas with other local teachers?

3 Teaching students of varying abilities

This chapter looks at how you can ensure that you teach students of all abilities effectively. First, it considers the issue of whether to teach in sets or mixed ability classes. It then considers the ways in which teachers can implement differentiation strategies, giving an example of how a topic can be taught to a mixed ability class. The rest of the chapter focuses first on less able students and then on more gifted students, giving examples of activities designed to ensure that they are motivated and achieve their full potential.

Setting versus mixed ability teaching

Wherever Geography is being taught, you face the challenge of ensuring that students of all abilities are inspired by the subject and given every opportunity to achieve their individual potential. In some schools, there is only one Geography class in each year group and students may cover a wide ability range. In those schools where there are several classes in each year group, they may be arranged in either mixed ability classes or in sets. The decision to set according to ability or to teach mixed ability groups may be a whole school or departmental issue. There are benefits and problems associated with each approach.

Setting brings together students of similar ability and allows the pace and style of learning to be geared towards each set being taught. This can make planning easier and allows resources to be matched to students' needs. The pace and style of learning and the content coverage can be varied, with appropriate activities being planned to extend top sets fully, while appropriate support can be provided to lower sets. It may also be possible to reduce the class size of lower sets in order to attend to individual needs more effectively.

However, setting brings its problems. Students may seem to be of similar ability, but their individual strengths and weaknesses may be very different and must be recognised. Within the same set, some students may possess excellent mapwork and presentation skills, but struggle when trying to understand conceptual ideas. Others may have excellent conceptual understanding but a mental block whenever a map is placed in front of them. It is important to ensure that a 'whole class' approach does not prevent you from providing individual support and, if necessary, differentiated tasks, in order to help students to make progress. Setting increases the risk of creating a situation where students with either behavioural or academic problems, or both, are grouped together. It may become self-fulfilling, with students performing to the level of the set they are in. Well-motivated students in lower sets may feel discouraged, while others may feel uncomfortable in top sets if they feel that they cannot meet perceived expectations or the pace or styles of learning do not suit them.

The use of mixed ability groups can resolve many of these issues. When it is used effectively, mixed ability grouping can provide appropriate opportunities for all students. Many Geography teachers manage it successfully, deploying a wide range of teaching methods and using differentiated teaching materials. However, it is a challenge to ensure that it is adequately resourced and that differentiation is practised, as failure to do so can reduce the achievement of some students (often the most and least able).

Mixed ability grouping enables students to progress at their own pace, reducing competition and ensuring that they are not 'labelled'. It gives everyone access to a common learning experience in Geography and does not restrict opportunities for learning. It encourages teaching and assessment in relation to individual needs and potential of students. It allows them to be encouraged and stimulated by others. Keen and enthusiastic geographers can act as models for others by setting standards and can enhance their own learning by explaining or discussing their work with others. Small group learning activities can be organised where individuals are carefully put together in order for each to benefit from their different combined talents.

The effective teaching of mixed ability groups makes large demands on the teacher, as the planning, preparing and acquiring of appropriate geographical resource materials requires much time and effort. You will have to spend significant amounts of time preparing for and responding to individual students, which could have a detrimental effect on levels of class control. There is also the danger of using inappropriate class teaching or whole class worksheets, and special needs support is not easy to provide when those requiring it are not timetabled together.

Differentiation

Differentiation is a planned process of intervention in the classroom to maximise potential on the basis of individual needs. It is an important method of ensuring that all students have access to the Geography curriculum. It should be in place not only to support those who are weak and to challenge the more able, but also to provide appropriate activities to those in between. Whether you are teaching Geography to a mixed ability class or a set, it is a useful strategy to differentiate the work which students are asked to do. However, it is within a mixed ability situation that it is especially important to ensure that effective differentiation strategies are implemented. It is unlikely that many students will achieve their full potential if you constantly use whole class activities.

There are three key ways in which you can develop differentiation strategies:

- differentiation by **resource**:
  - readability levels of textbooks and worksheets;
  - range and type of resource materials used;
  - varying use of ICT resources;
- differentiation by **task**:
  - variety of planned tasks and outcomes;
  - matching tasks to levels of ability and individual strengths and weaknesses;
  - linking tasks to the Geography assessment objectives and differentiating within the class in terms of assessment objectives;
  - identifying an essential core, together with reinforcement and extension activities – it is essential for teachers to be clear in terms of what they want all, most and some students to achieve;
- differentiation by **support level**:
  - support from the teacher or other adults;
  - peer support;
  - support from ICT resources.

To achieve differentiation you could use a range of approaches to meet the needs of students within the teaching group:

- You could use a variety of materials in any one lesson (e.g. photographs, newspaper extracts, atlas maps) to reinforce the content. Materials used need not be common to all individuals and groups. Additional resources can be introduced during the lesson to extend more able students.
- You could use a variety of teaching and learning styles (e.g. groupwork, independent learning, role play, decision-making exercises). This caters for all types of students, makes Geography more interesting and varied and reinforces different skills.
- When groups are used, you should structure them carefully. In some cases, a mixture of abilities could be grouped and the tasks within the group divided carefully within it such that each group produces a similar outcome. In other cases, groups could consist of students of

similar ability and the required outcome should reflect the learning needs of each different group.
- You should make additional resources available for students to allow independent learning and extension activity (e.g. geographical magazines, videos, access to selected websites).
- You should make the objectives and outcomes clear to students, particularly the essential core learning.
- You should give opportunities for repeat practice of geographical skills and concepts where it is required by individual students.

Flexibility is essential when you plan differentiated tasks. No single learning style or grouping of individuals is correct for every student, or for the whole time. Students need to be in different groupings in different situations. The appropriateness of any grouping will be governed by the type of task set, the individual learning needs and the space and resources available.

There are many occasions when a student needs individual instruction. This may be to master a particular mapping skill or gain an understanding of a challenging geographical concept. However, these sessions should not be particularly long, as short spells of intense effort are usually more effective than spending a long time on a task which is proving difficult. While working individually with a student may be useful, it does cut down the time an individual can learn through social interaction and much consideration should be given to achieving a balance when planning. It is often true that, when working with others in carefully selected groups, students will learn faster than if they are working in isolation.

Suggested approaches to teaching urbanisation to a mixed ability class

Most examination syllabuses require a knowledge of the location of expanding cities in developing countries and an understanding of the causes and impacts of rural to urban migration. This topic:
- offers plenty of opportunity for you to involve students in atlas work and activities involving the presentation of numerical data;
- enables students to work in groups using a variety of resources, including the Internet.

You can introduce the topic by providing your class with lists of some of the world's largest cities along with their current population, a projected population figure and a figure from a previous year. Students could work individually or in pairs to produce a map to show these cities and you could ask them to display the population figures in an effective way. Differentiation could be achieved by resource, task and level of support.

Confident and able individuals could be supplied with atlases and detailed statistical information, including not only city sizes in key years but also details of the changing percentage of rural and urban population in different parts of the world. You could encourage them to produce composite maps, using high level mapping skills to show increasing city sizes and urban percentage in developing countries.

You could give students who are less confident in working with maps and statistics a limited amount of information, perhaps fewer cities or only two base years to deal with (a projected figure may be hard for them to understand). Guidance could be provided in the form of a partially completed map, on which they need to find and label the cities shown by a dot on the map. It may be necessary to provide much support, so that they can identify them using an atlas or a wall map. Rather than presenting the information about population size on the map, they might be more capable of graphing their figures using a basic technique such as a bar chart for each year, though some could be encouraged to create a method of showing the information about both years on one graph framework.

Clearly the essential core knowledge to be gained is that most of these cities are now in developing countries, where an increasing number of people are migrating from rural areas. All students should gain this knowledge, irrespective of their task.

Having introduced the topic, you could then divide the class into groups in order to consider the causes and impacts of this urban growth. A variety of items of stimulus material of different levels of complexity can be used (e.g. photographs of both urban and rural areas in developing countries, newspaper articles outlining conditions in developing cities especially in the squatter settlement, videos showing footage of developing cities, textbooks, guidance on appropriate websites). Tasks can either vary according to ability groupings or be common to all groups if they contain a range of differing abilities.

For example, annotated push–pull diagrams can be produced by groups of students of varying abilities. Students tend to work very effectively when given the task of researching and producing a resource which visually displays the reasons for migrating (both pulls and pushes) and the conditions migrants face when they arrive in the cities. Initially, they extract appropriate factual material from the varied resources which they are given. Those who are more literate are often quite content to read and interpret complex materials such as newspaper articles. Weaker readers can use the evidence from photographs, enabling them to contribute to a discussion about conditions in squatter settlements. All students should be able to become involved in searching for appropriate websites, with those who are less confident in the use of ICT being schooled in the use of Internet search engines by those who are more experienced in their use. All members of the group tend to get involved in producing the work for display, the art work being proudly produced by those who often find difficulty in writing, under the close direction of other group members who ensure that all factual details are included in the annotation.

Supporting less able students
Success in Geography for less able students
All students have a range of strengths and weaknesses in their profiles of abilities. Strategies which you can use to identify those who are less able, along with their strengths and weaknesses, include:
- the use of benchmark data;
- information which has been gathered in previous schools and/or years;
- liaison with the learning support team.

However, significant aspects of a student's profile of abilities will quickly be revealed within the classroom, and it will be helpful for you to identify their levels of competence in a broad range of skills used in Geography (e.g. linguistic, logical, mathematical, spatial and personal–social skills). Such a summary of the unique individual pattern of development of each student's abilities will contribute to a fuller picture of their overall needs. This will enable appropriate targeting of activities and teaching strategies so that effective learning can take place. If an individual's primary problem is in literacy it is often worth focusing on that. Remedying reading problems and ensuring that resource materials and worksheets used are within the reading age of the student may help you to eradicate other problems such as poor motivation and antisocial behaviour.

When you prepare learning materials it is important to:
- plan a series of short structured tasks;
- make sentences short and simple;
- avoid difficult negative and passive constructions;
- avoid using unnecessary technical vocabulary unless it is absolutely necessary and try to use words familiar to students of their age;
- provide a glossary of important geographical words and phrases;
- repeat important words or ideas;
- avoid including too great a density of facts;
- spread out the resources, making it easy to follow and clear to see in print which is not too small or squashed together;
- avoid newspaper format (i.e. columns), as it is more difficult to follow than standard text;
- put the tasks together and make them stand out (e.g. by drawing a box around them) – do not hide tasks away so they are difficult to find amongst graphics;

- avoid using graphics, photographs and maps which reproduce badly or converting colour resources such as detailed maps into indistinct black and white versions;
- ensure that tasks are not too difficult and that success can be achieved;
- make the text personal and within students' own experience if possible.

Motivating the less able

It is obvious that effective learning in Geography only takes place when students, whether more or less able, are motivated to do well. The approach and attitude of their teacher are instrumental in them being positive towards the subject. Teaching and learning strategies need to be carefully thought out, varied and capable of retaining interest (e.g. individual, paired and group work, written work and activities, tasks using varied resources, imaginative ideas such as geographical games and puzzles).

It is unlikely that less able students will achieve their potential if you:
- make everything as difficult as possible;
- teach them things which they have failed at before, especially if similar teaching strategies are used;
- make lessons boring and repetitive;
- are negative in feedback when assessing their work and cover it with red ink;
- expect them to fail and expresses surprise when they succeed;
- emphasise their weaknesses and mistakes, never their strengths;
- compare them unfavourably with others in the class or with their siblings.

Teacher activity 3.1

How would you ensure that you provide each of these three 15-year-old students with a positive learning experience?

Maria is always keen to join in discussion in class and enjoys taking a leading role in group discussion activities and simulations. She sometimes gets so involved that others dislike working with her in a group situation and are unhappy arguing against her point of view. However, she gets much less involved in written work and her reading age is low. Her ability to concentrate on tasks involving both reading and writing is poor and she soon becomes frustrated and disruptive.

Augusto is a fluent reader and he has an enquiring mind, although he is reluctant to join in any discussion or group activities. Much of his written work is poorly presented and he often fails to elaborate on his brief answers. He loves working with maps of various kinds and can often be found in the library with an atlas.

Gurpal finds concentration in the classroom very difficult and she does not settle down to many types of work quickly. She is content to neatly copy out text, pictures and maps from worksheets and textbooks, but understands and retains little when tested either in written form or orally.

In reading about these three teenagers, it is the differences between them which are more striking than any similarities. It is equally obvious that they all have considerable difficulties which need to be overcome in order to motivate them to achieve their potential in Geography. However, while it is important that you recognise and cater for individual differences in all your students, this does not rule out the identification of common characteristics in those who appear to struggle in Geography lessons. What then are the common characteristics which may be identified in students commonly described as 'less able'? Experience suggests that reading, writing and number work can be identified as the basic skills which cause most problems across the curriculum, and Geography is no exception. In Geography lessons, other problems include limited concentration and retention of factual details, difficulties in handling abstract ideas, generalisations and concepts and difficulty in accepting alternative viewpoints. As it is unlikely that all problems will be experienced by each student it is important for you to identify initially the learning problems faced by an individual. Only then can you select and implement appropriate activities in order to help prepare them and motivate them to succeed.

Suggested approaches to teaching volcanoes and earthquakes to those who are less able

Plate tectonics is a very popular topic and the study of volcanoes and earthquakes is an example of 'disaster Geography' which is often enjoyed by students. One aspect of its appeal is that there is a large amount of visual material available showing the impacts of tectonic activity. It is not hard for anyone to imagine what life must be like in areas threatened by these natural hazards. It is more of a challenge, however, to teach the causes and distribution of volcanoes and earthquakes to students whose conceptual understanding is weak.

Example 1: introducing the impacts of earthquakes

It is useful to begin by using a variety of stimulus materials which focus on a single recent event. You could use video footage or still photographs, with easy-to-understand stories about how the event affected a number of people.

Here is an example of an email which you could use to begin a study of earthquakes.

```
From: Charlene Spencer [cspencer@hotmail.com]
Sent: 28 February 2001 23:18
To: Clive Spencer; Hayley Spencer; James Pitman-
Forsythe
Subject: Earthquake

Hello all. I didn't know if you had heard about the
earthquake but I am OK. It was all very odd. At
first I thought something had blown up, or a lorry
had crashed into the building. It went on for about
30-45 seconds so we left the building. Everything,
including the floor, shook violently. Some parts of
the buildings downtown have collapsed and a few
cars were crushed. Cracks have appeared in some of
the older buildings. Some buildings like the
library have shut. All the books were knocked onto
the floor. It was a force 7 earthquake and the
centre of it was 30 miles underground.
```

Note that the wording of the email is simple and should not provide too many difficulties for students who struggle with reading. You could read it out if necessary and encourage discussion about what happens to people in buildings when earthquakes occur. You could ask students to underline words which they do not understand (e.g. force 7) to introduce key concepts. This could form the basis of an initial study before resources such as photographs and video clips are used to look at other effects. While newspaper cuttings are often used for this purpose, I would suggest that it may be more effective to let students produce their own newspaper articles. Working individually, in pairs or in groups, they would need to be given very clear instructions so they included a headline, the story, picture(s) and a map to show where the earthquake occurred.

Example 2: recognising and explaining the distribution of tectonic activity

While recognising the effects of tectonic activity is a fairly straightforward exercise for students of any ability, many of limited ability struggle to describe their spatial distribution and explain it. If you involve them in practical activities they are more likely to be able to understand the significance of the boundaries between the earth's tectonic plates.

You could easily produce a resource similar to Figure 5 and give students a copy of the sheet in order to cut out the shapes and assemble them jigsaw fashion to produce a world map on which land and sea can be coloured and plates named. Using a map showing locations where volcanoes have erupted and earthquakes occurred they can then produce a traced overlay. This should help them to see that tectonic activity generally occurs on plate boundaries.

The joins between the jigsaw pieces may help them to see plate boundaries as lines of weaknesses and the significance of this will need to be emphasised. Some students may only be able to think in terms of lava escaping through the gap between the plates while others may be more able to grasp the underlying processes which occur due to plate movement.

It is useful to guide students by using a structured format such as in the following activities.

Student activity 3.2

Look at the map of the world which you have made. Put a tick next to the four of these sentences which you think are true.

The plates are moving slowly.

The plates fit tightly together.

Volcanoes are only found on the coast.

Volcanoes and earthquakes are mostly found where the plates join.

Plates are made of land and sea.

Earthquakes only happen where it is hot.

Earthquakes are mostly found in the centre of plates.

This should provide a simple start. Students could be asked to copy out the correct statements if required, to further emphasise the relationship between plate boundaries and tectonic activity.

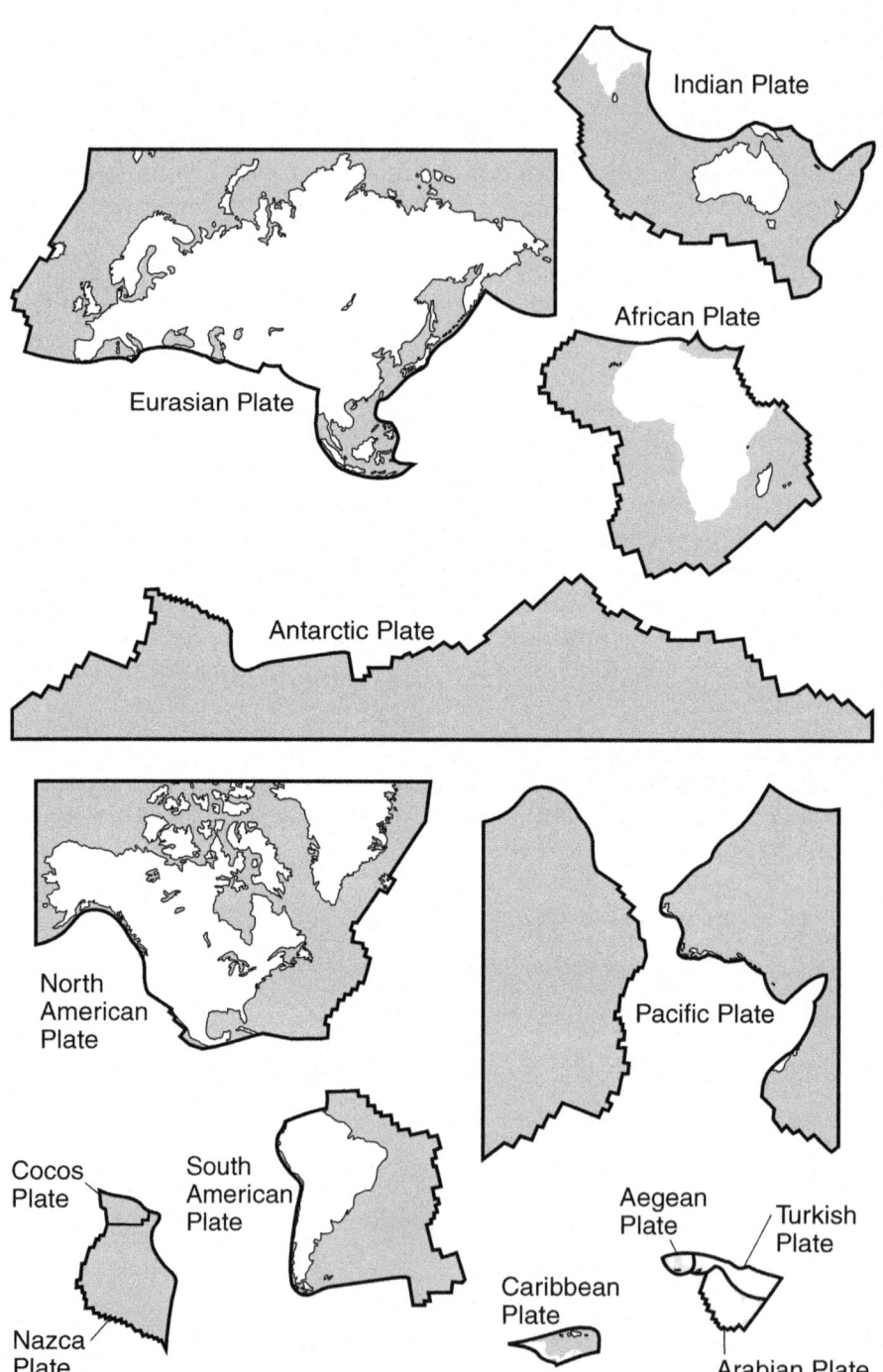

Figure 5: Tectonic plates jigsaw map

Look at this diagram, which shows what happens when plates move towards each other.

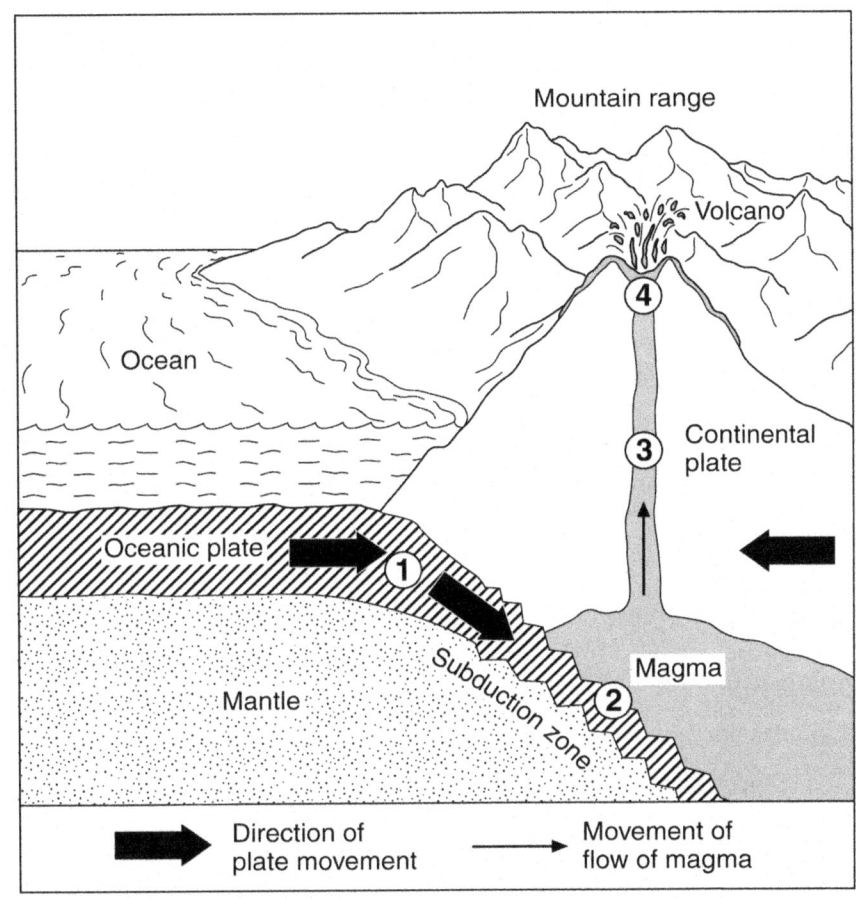

Figure 6: A destructive plate margin (Source: OCR Geography A 1586 Papers 1 and 2 June 2000)

Which numbers on the diagram match with these labels?

Rock is melted and turned into magma = Number _____

The plates are moving slowly towards each other = Number _____

Lava flows out of a volcano = Number _____

The magma is pushed through a weakness in the earth's crust = Number _____

Notes

- The complexity of the statements will need to match the ability of the students.
- The use of technical terms like plates, magma, lava and volcano are important here. You will need to define them.
- While the purpose of this activity is to explain the occurrence of volcanoes at plate boundaries it should also reinforce what has been learnt about their location and distribution.

Student activity 3.4

You now need to write about where in the world volcanoes and earthquakes happen. You will need to look at your map and answers to Student activities 3.2 and 3.3.

Firstly, you need to use the map to write about where volcanoes and earthquakes happen:

My map shows me that volcanoes and earthquakes happen ....
.... (Where are they mostly found on the map? Make sure you write about plates.)

An example of a volcano is ....

This volcano erupted ....
....
(Where did it erupt? Is it where two plates join? If so, which ones?)

An example of an earthquake is ....

This earthquake happened ....
....
(Where did it happen? Is it where two plates join? If so, which ones?)

Now you should write about what makes the volcanoes erupt:

A volcano erupts where plates join because ....
....
(Look at the labels for the diagram in Student activity 3.3. Write them as your answer in the correct order.)

Notes

- The use of the writing frame provides appropriate guidance for students in structuring their writing. Less able students often experience difficulty in structuring and sequencing work. Writing frames are particularly useful to help them to do this and they also make it clear what factual information should be included.

- The main purpose of Student activity 3.4 is consolidation, as students are reinforcing their understanding by looking back at previous work.

Example 3: making a model of a volcano
This is a fun exercise which students of any age enjoy. There are many ways to make a model of a volcano and the activity will help them become familiar with its shape and features.

Student activity 3.5

The activity will certainly stimulate learning about what really makes a volcano erupt!

You will need the following equipment for the quick demonstration:

a small plastic bottle
1/4 cup (60 ml) water
1 tablespoon (15 ml) baking soda
1/4 cup (60 ml) vinegar
a small piece of toilet tissue
a few drops of red food colouring
a few drops of liquid dishwashing detergent

For the display model, you will also need dark grey and red modelling clay and model trees, etc. for the surroundings.

How to make your volcano
1 For the quick demonstration, put the plastic bottle in your sink. For the display model, build a mountain with modelling clay around the bottle, using grey clay to build the cone, and adding red clay in rivulets down the side to look like lava streams.
2 Put the water, detergent, food colouring and vinegar in the bottle.
3 Wrap the baking soda in the toilet tissue and twist the ends to make a little packet.
4 When you are ready to make the volcano erupt, drop the packet of soda into the bottle. The acid of the vinegar and the base of the baking soda combine to foam, froth and erupt.

Source: http://rockhoundingar.com/pebblepups/volcano.html

Providing a challenge in Geography for gifted students

Whether taught in sets or mixed ability groups, students who are gifted in Geography should be given every opportunity to achieve their full potential. Such individuals are likely to:

- understand concepts well and be able to apply their understanding to new situations in order to make interpretations, develop hypotheses, reach conclusions and explore solutions;
- understand and be able to explain complex processes and inter-relationships (e.g. within and between physical and human environments);
- communicate knowledge, ideas and understanding, both orally and in written form, using subject-specific terminology;
- be competent and confident in using the wide range of visual resources required in Geography – aerial photographs, satellite images, maps of different types and scales and geographical information systems (GIS);
- take part readily in role-play situations or simulations and enjoy contributing to outdoor fieldwork;
- have well thought out opinions on issues such as the environment and the inequalities of life in different places.

You need to be challenging and supportive in order for such students to be given every opportunity to develop the breadth and depth of their geographical experiences and the quality of their responses. The following strategies are useful:

- Provide studies at a variety of scales (local, regional, national and global) and contexts (countries at varying levels of economic development) and on a variety of topics (e.g. physical, human Geography and environmental issues).
- Provide more difficult and complex resources which allow students to develop high level skills.
- Ensure that the tasks based on the resources demand analysis and synthesis and involve the communication of outcomes in both written and oral forms.
- Give students opportunities to work independently by using an enquiry approach where you provide guidance rather than instruction. This should involve the collection and representation of data from primary and secondary sources, its analysis and the drawing of conclusions. In this way, gifted students can be encouraged to show initiative and independence of mind.
- Assemble a range of resources to enhance further study. These should include satellite images, aerial photographs of different types, maps of different scales, types and locations, and a wide range of ICT resources including Internet access and video materials.

- Provide opportunities, both locally and further afield, to enhance geographical learning by the use of field studies.

Suggested approaches to teaching variations in agricultural land use

These suggested activities form part of a teaching programme on agricultural land use where students are required to describe and explain the distribution of farming types in a developing country. They are designed to develop higher order skills such as analysis, synthesis and hypothesising by the use of statistical and cartographic materials.

India is referred to here as an exemplar as clear spatial variations in agricultural production and output can be related to factors such as relief and climate. However, you could use any country provided that up-to-date materials are available. The following two websites provide a wealth of statistical material relating to Indian agricultural output which can be incorporated into student worksheets:

- www.indiaagristat.com/indian/agriculture
- www.economywatch.com/database/agriculture.htm

Initially, you should locate the chosen country and outline its regional variations in relief and climate. This provides an ideal opportunity for the use of atlas maps of various types.

Students then complete tasks such as those in Student activities 3.6 to 3.10.

Student activity 3.6

You should provide students with information on the climatic requirements of some of the main crops grown in the country being studied. For example, rice and wheat are important crops in India. For a high yield of rice, Indian farmers need 130 wet days, with an average daily precipitation of over 8 mm. In contrast, wheat farmers produce high yields where there are 125 wet days, with an average daily precipitation of around 4 mm.

Having looked at the regional differences in climate in India, students should use their atlas maps and discuss the climatic areas where they would expect most wheat and rice to be grown. They should be able to hypothesise which Indian regions are likely to be major rice and wheat farming areas.

You should now give students a map showing the main crops grown in different parts of India to use, along with their atlas map showing spatial variations in rainfall. They should be asked to show if there is a relationship between total annual rainfall in India and the main crops grown by using an overlay map.

Overlay maps will need to be carefully constructed if they are to be used to determine any relationship which exists. Students may be able to work out for themselves that a base map showing crops in different colours with a choropleth overlay of rainfall will work best, although it is likely that you will have to give some guidance.

Using their completed maps they should be able to observe relationships between precipitation and main crop types. In addition, they should be encouraged to look at the distribution of wheat and rice and comment on how accurate their first thoughts were (Student activity 3.6).

Student activity 3.8

Using tables which show the yield of wheat and rice and the annual rainfall in different states in India, students could construct scatter graphs and/or calculate Spearman's rank correlation coefficients to test the relationship between rainfall and the yields of rice and wheat.

The interpretation of scatter graphs should be straightforward for most individuals, although the statistical test will be more challenging. It is important that they interpret the graph and correlation coefficients rather than just mechanically produce them, and that they understand the significance of any correlation which exists.

Maps showing the states of India should be available to help students to see the spatial variation. If necessary, yields and rainfall could be plotted using choropleth mapping or proportional symbols as an alternative to the statistical test.

This task will reinforce the significance of precipitation as a major factor in agricultural land use and provide students with an explanation of relationships they observed in Student activity 3.7.

It should now be very clear that precipitation is one of the main factors which can be used to explain the variation in agricultural land use in India. However, other significant physical factors include temperature, soil and relief.

Students could work in groups to find out what effect these factors have on the distribution of rice and wheat growing in India. This would present an ideal opportunity for further work using atlases, although the use of Internet sites could be encouraged here. If appropriate, you could ask groups to present their findings to the class.

This exercise involves collaborative research and oral feedback. It may be possible to divide the task and ask each group to research a particular factor or crop and report back.

Student activity 3.10

Students should now be able to write an account which describes and explains the distribution of agricultural land use in India. You could encourage them to draw an annotated sketch map summarising the information.

 LOOKING BACK

This chapter has emphasised the need to recognise that, in all classes, it is inevitable that there will a mixture of students who possess different abilities. While this mixture will be greater in some circumstances than others, you must always provide appropriate opportunities for all students. Look back at some of the ideas in this chapter and ask yourself the following questions:
◆ Do you use a wide enough range of teaching methods and differentiated materials within your classes?
◆ Do you always think about differentiation by task and resource or do you simply rely on providing different levels of support for students?
◆ Are you giving your most able students appropriate and stimulating challenges?
◆ Are your least able students achieving their full potential?

4 Using a variety of teaching strategies

All teachers and students use a variety of teaching and learning styles. This chapter gives examples of teaching and learning activities which incorporate different styles, focusing particularly on active learning. It also looks at how textbooks, ICT and other equipment can be drawn on as resources to support your teaching.

Active or passive students?

Learning takes place in different ways, including visual learning (learning by seeing), auditory learning (learning by hearing) and kinaesthetic learning (learning by doing). You should make use of many different activities which involve each type of learning in the Geography classroom, especially those which involve 'learning by participation'. This will ensure that your lessons remain exciting and stimulating. It is also important to remember that the initial contact for learning is made in the classroom, so the classroom environment is very important, and must be welcoming and attractive.

While there will always be scope in the Geography classroom for the didactic approach and the individual use of textbooks by students, you should take every opportunity to adopt an approach which involves learning by thinking and participating. Some topics clearly lend themselves to a specific approach. However, whether the approach you use is one which is distinctive to Geography alone (e.g. fieldwork investigations, geographical games and simulations) or one which is shared by other subjects (e.g. problem solving, discussion and groupwork), variety will ensure that, over time, the needs of all students are met.

Teaching styles appropriate to Geography include:
- didactic approaches, including presentation from teachers and other students;
- problem-solving and decision-making exercises;
- discussion in pairs, groups or the whole class;
- geographical games and simulation activities;
- resource-based learning activities involving the use of maps, graphs, photographs and other visual stimuli;

- individual, paired, group or whole class fieldwork exercises;
- observation of activities, events, photographs and the environment.

Associated learning activities include:
- listening and watching;
- reading, writing and word processing;
- problem solving;
- planning, investigating and gathering data, both in and out of the classroom;
- talking and discussing;
- role play and decision making;
- reading and interpretation of maps, graphs and diagrams;
- presentation of data in various forms, including maps, annotated sketches and diagrams;
- learning and recalling information;
- analysing and drawing conclusions from sources of information;
- evaluation and self-review of investigations and other forms of completed work.

Work which can be produced for assessment includes written tasks, visual display work (including maps, diagrams, graphs, posters and wall displays) and oral presentations (both individually and as part of a group presentation).

Whatever teaching styles and learning activities you use, it is vital to plan for students to achieve progression by:
- building up from the stage where they are using a limited geographical vocabulary to one where they are using a wider range of geographical vocabulary, precisely and with confidence;
- extending their geographical knowledge of places from a basic knowledge of a limited number of places, particularly in the local area, to a more detailed knowledge of a wider range of areas and an understanding of the links between them;
- developing their understanding of physical and human processes, to enable explanations to be given as well as descriptions;
- explaining events and geographical phenomena, using with increasing confidence abstract ideas and models of real situations;
- extending their use of simple drawings, maps and diagrams such that, where appropriate, a wider range of more complex maps, diagrams and graphs are used with confidence to represent geographical information;
- becoming less reliant on guided practical activities in the field, working independently outside the classroom in order to plan and undertake individual enquiry.

While all your students have their preferred learning styles, there are a number of widely recognised differences to look out for which may be the result of gender. In general, boys are speculative thinkers and their hands go up quickly in lessons, while girls are reflective thinkers, wanting to consider alternatives before an answer is offered. Boys tend not to be as good listeners as girls and are prepared to read less. Boys are less likely to enjoy writing for its own sake, preferring to write for a purpose and enjoying short specific tasks such as problem solving. Girls often do better in open-ended tasks which require cooperation, and tend to be more organised in their work. Instant praise is important to all students, boys in particular responding well to regular target setting.

Teacher activity 4.1

Do you teach both boys and girls? If so, what differences do you notice in their learning styles?

How do you think gender differences are likely to influence the way in which boys and girls approach the following three activities:
- a computer simulation exercise which involves decision making about land use on a commercial farm;
- the production of a wall display, based on research carried out on the causes and effects of deforestation in Amazonia;
- the use of maps and graphs to display information collected on a field trip to the Central Business District (CBD) of an urban area?

Examples of active learning activities in Geography

It would be impossible to cover in detail all teaching strategies and learning activities in this chapter. However, I shall describe and give examples of the following different approaches, all of which I have used successfully with classes of different sizes, ages and abilities:
- guided conversations;
- back to back conversations;
- where shall I stand?
- newsroom;
- card-sorting activities;
- activities developing thinking skills;
- cooperative groupwork.

Be prepared to experiment; you might find your classroom a little more noisy and lively than usual, but you will know that all students will be active and therefore more likely to learn!

Guided conversations

In pairs, students take it in turns to converse about a given topic (about two minutes each). For example, one might explain how and where a river carries out erosion, while his partner explains how and where deposition occurs. The knowledge base could either be previous learning or the results of a piece of simple research from a textbook or other source. They then join together with another pair and take it in turns to relate to the other pair what their partner has just said. A debrief then follows where what has been remembered and forgotten is identified.

This exercise develops listening skills and is useful for both revising a topic and helping students to understand new ideas and concepts. You could use the idea with any age and ability groups and it would be appropriate when studying any topic.

Back to back

Students sit in pairs, back to back. One has a picture in front of them, for example a picture of a coastal landform such as a natural arch. They describe the feature as clearly as possible to their partner who has to sketch it on a blank piece of paper from their partner's description. The original picture and completed drawing are then compared and both students decide how the original could have been described to produce greater clarity. If required, this description can then be written down and an annotated sketch produced.

This is a useful exercise to introduce the study of landforms of a particular type or in a specific area, encouraging clarity of description and providing practice in sketching skills. Further work would introduce relevant terminology and focus on processes and explanation.

Where shall I stand?

This is a useful exercise to carry out from time to time when you are expecting students to be able to identify where they are, what they are or what opinions they hold.

For example, if the classroom represents the world (or a specific country) students are each given a card with the name of a country (or place within a country) printed on it. They then have to collaborate with each other to work out where to stand relative to each other. This activity could introduce the place being studied and atlases could be used if necessary. Another use of the idea would be to recap knowledge of a map.

Alternatively, you could ask students to stand in a specific part of the classroom according to what is written on their card. For example, in an activity concerned with classification of types of economic activity, those with cards showing pictures of primary activities could stand by the blackboard, those with secondary activities by the door and those with tertiary activities by the window.

Another variation involves laying out a straight line whose ends represent extreme opinions, for example views strongly for or against a specific development such as deforestation of an area of tropical rainforest. Again, you could give out pre-prepared cards and ask students to stand in the appropriate position according to the opinion and strength of feeling of the interest group represented. Those representing the indigenous tribe and conservationists from the USA are both likely to disagree with the development, but interesting discussions ensue about who would feel most strongly.

Newsroom

In this activity, students simulate the process of preparing a timed news item for radio or television. It works best if students are organised into groups such that each one can take on a particular role, therefore contributing not only to the putting together of the item but also to the finished presentation. You should give groups a set time to put together their presentation. A useful addition is for you to introduce at intervals the latest developments. This exercise is ideal to use when looking at events such as earthquakes, volcanic eruptions, floods and extreme weather events (e.g. hurricanes). Group members could take on the roles of newscaster and reporters at the scene, while others represent the experts who are interviewed to explain why the event occurred, or people who have been affected by the tragedy. If the event is current, group research could be incorporated; alternatively, textbook case studies can be used to obtain information.

Card-sorting activities

The use of cards as a learning tool can be carried out by individual students, pairs or groups. Cards are particularly useful for matching exercises (e.g. terms with definitions, descriptions with diagrams, pictures with maps) or sequencing exercises (e.g. following a route on a map, developing an understanding of processes such as processes of weathering or tectonic activity). For whatever purpose the cards are used, the exercise involves students in thinking and discussion, thus aiding understanding. Being able to sort the cards, discuss their arrangements with others, then reposition them following discussion means that success is more likely. This is useful for those who may lack confidence and become demotivated by repeatedly crossing out errors. Students need only commit their answers to paper when they are satisfied that they are correct and are therefore able to take a pride in their work.

Developing thinking skills

Many Geography teachers are involved in developing activities which encourage thinking skills, incorporating decision making, working together and problem solving. They have the added dimension of asking students to consider not only what they learnt but how they learnt it (i.e. the process which they followed to reach their conclusion). These activities include living graphs, mysteries, sequencing, mind movies and memory maps.

This example involves the sequencing of events in the eruption of a volcano. It is a simple exercise which you can easily adapt and use when looking at the shaping of any natural landform (e.g. a coastal headland or a waterfall). Students are presented with cards showing the six stages in the evolution of a volcano (Figure 7) which they are asked to arrange in sequential order. This works best as a paired exercise so discussion can take place. The labels which accompany the pictures could be omitted and students asked to produce labels to describe what is happening. Alternatively, you could give them the labels on separate cards and ask them to match them with the pictures before the sequencing exercise.

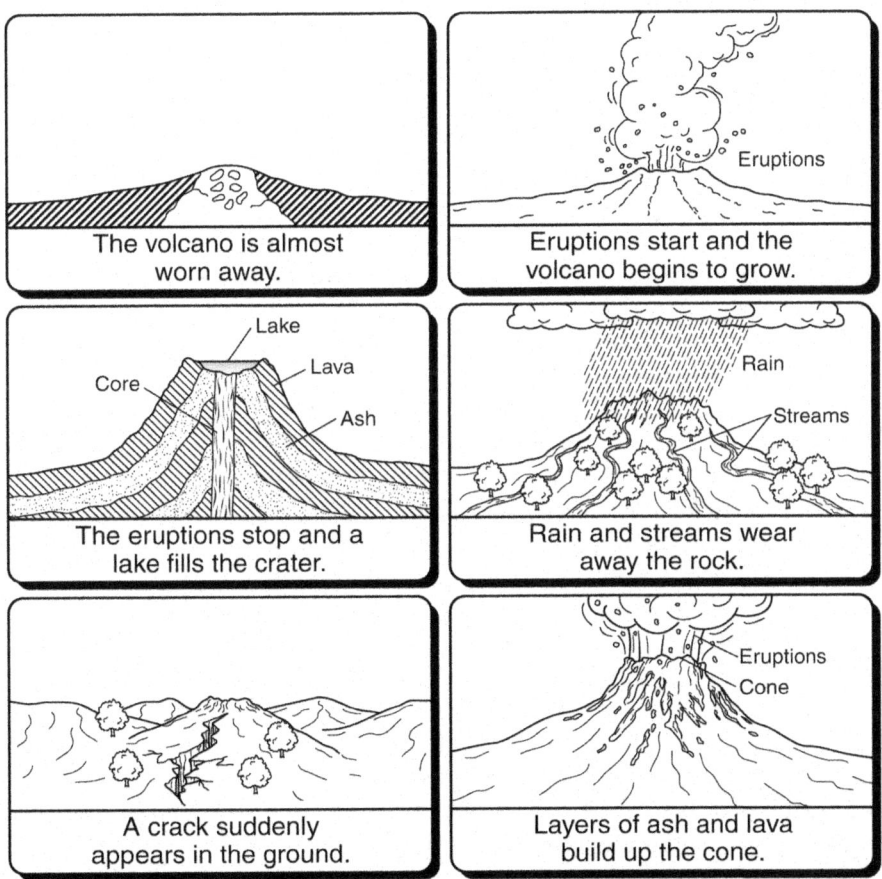

Figure 7: Volcano evolution sequence

You can see further examples of activities which develop thinking skills at:

- www.geoworld.co.uk
- www.sln.org.uk/geography/thinking_through_geography.htm

Cooperative groupwork

Cooperative groupwork is an active teaching tool where students, operating together in small groups to achieve a common goal, can develop both their social and intellectual skills. While the interdependence of group members encourages the need for mutual support, you should structure activities such that individuals are encouraged to feel accountable by ensuring that every member of the group must, in some way, demonstrate achievement. It provides the scope for sensitive grouping that enables differentiation to be achieved. The interaction between individuals promotes social skills such as encouraging, listening, giving help, leadership and decision making. The approach is highly flexible and can involve a wide range of learning activities.

Suggested approach to teaching about the factors affecting the distribution of population

This is an example of an activity which is designed to involve students in collecting and organising information in groups, forming categories to classify the data, and using the data effectively. The processes involved mean that what is learnt is more likely to be retained. It creates an active learning environment and can be used with any topic where a data set is easily obtained.

- Stage 1 of the process, as always, should be to identify a focus for the activity along with objectives expressed in terms of skills, knowledge and understanding.
- Stage 2 involves the collection of the data set appropriate to the topic selected for study. The data set can be collected by students as a part of the exercise or produced by the teacher in advance. The data can take many forms (e.g. photographs, graphs, rock samples). However, there should be enough in number and variety to encourage wide-ranging responses. The items, once collected, need to be numbered or lettered and labelled.
- Stage 3 is the point at which the data set is examined and classified by students in groups, the results being shared with the whole class. This can be done by the teacher coordinating a class summary or by each group producing a resource such as a poster.
- Stage 4 involves students in using the categories identified in order to understand relationships within the area of study. When doing so, they may be able to obtain and use other items of data which belong to the categories which they have identified.

The following activity uses pictures of different types of landscape – some densely populated, others sparsely populated – to illustrate the factors which underlie the distribution of population.

Student activity 4.1

You should select between 20 and 30 pictures showing different types of landscape such as:

- mountains;
- a woodland area;
- arable farmland;
- desert sand dunes;
- a polar ice cap;
- marshland;
- part of a squatter settlement;
- a housing estate alongside a busy main road;
- a built-up area around a river crossing;
- an industrial area.

Clearly, this list is not exhaustive. It just gives examples of areas which vary in their population density for a variety of reasons. There are many other examples which you could provide by using magazines, postcards or photographs in a wall display. Alternatively, students could be asked to bring in pictures as part of an introduction to work on settlement. Photographs in text books could also be used for this exercise.

Once the pictures have been displayed, groups should be instructed to pick a small number which have a common link. Groupings would be likely to include areas:

- where few/lots of people live;
- which have cold/hot/wet/dry climates;
- which have high/low/steep/flat relief;
- which appear to be rich/poor;
- which are close to the coast/rivers/main roads;
- which have lots/small amounts of work.

How this is organised is flexible and will depend on the nature of the students. It is useful to start off by working in pairs, so that all students are involved at an early stage. Given a careful selection of pictures, they will all be able to pick some pictures with common links before joining together in larger groups where their ideas will be pooled. This should lead to a reporting back stage where it will be possible for you to use the suggested groupings to identify the factors responsible for variation in population density on both a local and global scale. The extent of teacher direction given here will depend on the needs of the students. In some cases, it may be possible for groups to set up and test hypotheses based on the data set along with maps showing the location of the photographs and influencing factors (e.g. climatic zones, major mountain areas, resource availability, communications etc). Alternatively, you could give students the help of a writing frame and more structured exercises as follow-up.

Teacher activity 4.2

Choose an appropriate topic. As part of a unit of work on that topic, plan a lesson which involves active learning. You could try out ideas from this chapter or you may have ideas of your own which involve students in learning by participation. It is always useful to share ideas with your colleagues. Why not try the activities out and ask a colleague to observe your lesson? You could then discuss the activity with your colleague and decide whether involving students in active learning has made the lesson interesting and worthwhile.

Strategies which use textbooks effectively

In many schools, the use of the textbook is the predominant activity in Geography classrooms, although unfortunately it is often perceived as an activity lacking in imagination and creativity. This may indeed be so, and those students who are treated to constant note-taking or comprehension exercises based on the set text can be excused if they feel that Geography has little of real interest to offer. You should not expect one textbook, or series of textbooks, to meet all the needs of students. The wealth of material within a textbook is not a substitute for good teaching, or an easy option for either teachers or students.

Despite this, there is no doubt that textbooks are an essential resource. They provide the appropriate factual information required and incorporate a wealth of resources and a series of structured exercises. It is up to the imaginative teacher to ensure that they are used creatively as a resource bank rather than followed slavishly. A good textbook provides the scope for you to use the text selectively and set activities based on it, together with other activities in the classroom.

The textbook alone may well provide self-contained homework tasks, and can be relied on to be the basis of work which needs to be set while the class is being covered by a non-specialist.

However, the skilled Geography teacher will recognise that, along with text, a textbook will contain resources of many types, including different types and scales of maps, colour photographs, aerial photographs, satellite images, statistics presented in both tabular and graph form, short newspaper and magazine extracts, cartoons and diagrams of different types and styles which can be used in many innovative ways. Given the variety and relevance of much of the material, it is useful to be able to be selective. Occasionally you can use the text and structured exercises, but supplement them by using resources in the book as a stimulus for skills-based exercises. For example, photographs of physical and human landscapes can be used by students to describe landscape features or develop field sketching skills, maps and aerial photographs can be used to describe and explain distributions, and statistical information and newspaper extracts can be used to stimulate discussion or even as the basis for decision-making exercises.

While most textbooks are produced with particular courses or age groups in mind, it is possible for you to use all textbooks with all age groups and abilities, providing of course it is the resource material which is being used rather than the text and the set exercises. Using textbook materials in this way will also provide opportunities for you to differentiate and provide relevant activities for all students. It is sometimes the case that the language of textbooks and nature of some of the set activities make learning difficult for those who are less able, particularly if their linguistic skills are poor. The repetitive use of such materials is likely to add to their sense of failure, unless you devise appropriate tasks to make the materials accessible. For gifted students, you may need to devise more challenging activities in order to develop their higher level skills.

Here are four examples of activities which can be devised using textbook materials.

Relating text and pictures
Pictures can be turned into text or text into diagrams or sketch maps. Using a photograph of a natural landscape (e.g. a glaciated valley), a written description, incorporating appropriate terminology, could be produced. Using photographs of housing in a squatter settlement and a high cost housing area, living conditions could be contrasted. Alternatively, text could be turned into pictures or labelled diagrams. For example, a labelled diagram of rainforest features could be produced from a standard description. Similarly, a diagram which helps students to understand the processes associated with the passage of a frontal system can be produced from a description of those processes.

Display of statistical material

Statistical material can be used to display data in an effective way to show either trends or distributions, followed by suitable analysis and explanation. For example, data showing the production of a particular primary or manufactured product from countries in a continent can be mapped and the distribution described. Annual output figures of the product from one or more of these countries can be graphed along with a description and/or comparison and explanation of any trends.

Use of writing frames

Writing frames can be used to provide a structure for students' own writing using the resources in a textbook. If carefully constructed, these help them to use geographical terminology and understand the key ideas and concepts, for example a piece of written work on the formation of a physical feature such as an oxbow lake. The design of the writing frame by the teacher should ensure that diagrams, photographs and text from the textbook need to be used to complete the written work and geographical terminology needs to be used and understood.

Creative writing

Creative writing can be based on material in textbooks which can be used to help students empathise with people or interest groups and present opinions from particular viewpoints. For example, students could use information in the textbook about plans for a change of land use, such as the construction of a new motorway, mine or quarry or airport. They could write letters to the local newspaper from local residents or contribute to a debate which highlights its impact on different members of the community.

Teacher activity 4.3

Choose any textbook together with an appropriate topic. For this topic, plan a lesson (or series of lessons) using at least two of the suggested activities. Why not try the activities out and evaluate them? If they are successful, they could be written into your scheme of work.

The use of ICT in Geography

ICT has considerable potential to make a significant contribution to learning in Geography and can be widely used while undertaking many types of work in Geography. These include fieldwork, research enquiries and investigations, as well as work assignments involving the interrogation and presentation of data. For many students, new technology provides motivation and interest, using a medium with which they are familiar. It is useful, therefore, to deploy as wide a range of ICT opportunities as possible, when working both inside and outside the Geography classroom.

It can contribute to learning by:

- enhancing skills of geographical enquiry both in and out of the classroom;
- extending skills of graphical, statistical and spatial analysis;
- enhancing the presentation of text, pictures, graphs and other materials;
- facilitating the understanding of geographical patterns, processes and relationships;
- enabling simulation or modelling of abstract or complex geographical systems or processes;
- providing access to a range of images of people, places and environments;
- communicating and exchanging information with people in other geographical areas.

The use of ICT can also support you as a teacher in a variety of ways. It can provide up-to-date knowledge, for example in the form of statistical and other information on countries, topical events and issues. You can save time by using the varied resources that can be easily accessed and downloaded, rather than creating them yourself. Such resources can be extremely flexible, as they can be simplified or extended to suit the needs of different students. Finally, you can use communications technology, such as video or PowerPoint presentations, to assist in the presentation of materials to students.

You should aim to include a variety of opportunities for learning within schemes of work. These could include the use of:

- Commercially produced geographical software (e.g. simulations of the location of settlement).
- Geographical information systems (GISs) for investigations, resource management simulation and development planning (e.g. a GIS might allow emergency planners to easily calculate emergency response times in the event of a natural disaster, or a GIS might be used to find wetlands which need protection from pollution).
- Cameras (e.g. digital cameras, video cameras and single use cameras) to obtain images while carrying out fieldwork – digital images can be scanned into work assignments or stored on CDs for future use.
- Data logging equipment (e.g. flow meters can be used for collecting data in the field, with dictaphones and tape recorders being useful for recording details of the data collected).

- Television and video recordings could be shown and role-play exercises could be recorded either on video or audio cassettes. Ceefax and Teletext systems are available on many television networks, providing an up-to-date and comprehensive information system.
- Communication in different ways using ICT (e.g. word processing text and using spreadsheets to present graphs). Overhead projector transparencies and/or PowerPoint presentations could be used by individuals and groups for presentations of work assignments.
- The Internet for individual or group research.
- Archive materials held on microfilm by, for example, local newspapers and public record offices, providing information for investigations in the local area.

The organisation and management of learning using ICT

Schools have access to different levels of ICT equipment. The availability of equipment within the school, along with its level of access to the Geography department, is a major factor influencing the extent to which it can be used to enhance learning and facilitate teaching.

When only a few machines are available, you need to give thought to integrating a number of different activities, such that those requiring the use of computers can be complemented by those which do not. The extent of teacher support required should also be considered, especially if other activities are to be integrated. It may be wise to develop ICT support materials which will enable students to work relatively independently at computers.

The time which it takes to give access to all students should also be considered, particularly if computers are being used for individual learning and integrated with other activities. Giving everyone equal access is vital and requires careful planning. A realistic policy is to try to develop short, sharply focused ICT activities. Where a suite of computers is available, it is often effective to work in pairs or threes rather than individually, with the added benefit of the discussion and cooperation which will enhance the work.

A suggested approach to using the Internet to undertake research on increasing agricultural output

In the 1960s, new crops were developed by cross-breeding plants to create high yielding varieties. This was known as the Green Revolution. Today, genetic modification goes one step further. Genes from one organism are isolated, then copied and inserted into another plant to give it new characteristics. It is argued by some scientists that this will enable plants to be developed to suit specific environments and food needs. This, they claim, will enable more food to be produced from less land, using less water and fewer chemicals. Other people worry that such developments are being pushed through without regard to their long-term impacts.

While much information can be found in textbooks about the Green Revolution, it is less likely that textbooks will contain materials relating to genetic modification of foods. As part of this scheme of work, there is therefore an ideal opportunity for information to be gathered from the Internet.

Student activity 4.2

Students could look at viewpoints on genetically modified foods on websites and research facts, figures and other evidence to support their arguments. They could work in groups to prepare arguments either for or against genetically modified foods in the form of a PowerPoint presentation. Alternatively, ICT could be deployed to present the facts and figures as a piece of publicity or as part of a magazine article.

These three examples of websites about the Green Revolution not only give factual information, but also offer different opinions about its impacts:

- www.indiaonestop.com/Greenrevolution.htm
- www.biotech-info.net/sour.html
- www.foodfirst.org/media/opeds/2000/4-greenrev.html

Here are examples of websites which your students can use to research the genetic modification of food. Those preparing arguments for genetic modification could look at:

- www.biotechknowledge.com
- www.agbioworld.com
- www.monsanto.com

Those preparing arguments against genetic modification could look at:

- www.wdm.org.uk/campaign/GMOs.htm
- www.foodfirst.org/progs/global/biotech

Choose a topic which would be ideal to use to involve students in Internet research. Any issue of international concern such as global warming, acid rain or deforestation would be an ideal choice, or there may be a significant national, regional or local issue in your country. Plan a series of lessons which involve students using material which is available on the Internet. They may or may not involve discussion or presentation, as Student activity 4.2 does, but make sure that active learning is taking place. Search for websites yourself to ensure that enough material is available and provide students with details of these on an information sheet.

LOOKING BACK

This chapter should have made you think about the importance of providing a variety of activities in your lessons. The classroom environment is the starting point for learning.

♦ Is your classroom always a place of interest to students? If not, how should this be addressed?

♦ Is your classroom inviting, colourful and friendly?

♦ Do you display student work prominently and change it regularly? Often students see display of work as a reward and are proud of getting their work displayed.

♦ Do your displays include visually appealing material which students will ask questions about?

♦ Do you take every opportunity to ensure that active learning is taking place in your classroom?

♦ How can you best use your textbooks and other resources effectively?

♦ In the 21st century, the use of ICT will become more important. Do you feel your ICT skills could be improved? If so, how will you address this?

5 The effective use of resource materials in Geography teaching

Amongst the many resource materials used by geographers, few would dispute the importance of maps of various types and scales. The use and interpretation of maps is, after all, the skill traditionally associated with the geographer. Maps are a major tool of the geographer and this should be acknowledged when constructing any scheme of work, yet they are just one type of resource which you can use to bring the subject alive.

The choice of resources which you use with students is of fundamental importance, both in their type, complexity and quantity. The following points should be carefully considered in their selection and use:

- Aim to employ a variety of resources with students, rather than constantly using the same type of resource.
- While variety is essential, you need to take care not to overload students with too many resources. Two or three resources used effectively would be more worthwhile than having six available which are only briefly considered.
- Devote care and time to the selection of resources which students will find interesting and therefore stimulating. For example, when teaching introductory mapwork and aerial photograph interpretation skills a map of their local area is always of more interest than one of a distant location.
- Ensure that the level of difficulty of resources used matches the needs of students. Care is needed to ensure that differentiation takes place in resource selection, both in the selection of resource type and degree of complexity.
- Try to keep resource materials up to date and always try to make use of modern technology and media. Black-and-white photographs of the damage caused by the floods in Lynmouth, UK, in 1952, along with articles from journals at the time, may provide an excellent case study to demonstrate ideas and concepts. However, why not consider a series of

video reports and website references to the flooding in Prague, Dresden and other parts of Eastern Europe in August 2002? The latter is likely to be much more stimulating and generate more interest amongst students.

- Try to avoid using resource materials simply for illustration or, worse still, for copying. Use them for skills development and active learning.

This chapter investigates how various resources – maps, photographs, information on current events and parents' involvement – can be obtained and suggests ways in which you can use a selection of them with students. (Note that other key resources such as textbooks and ICT have been discussed in Chapter 4.)

Maps as resources
Using atlases

Without doubt, the most commonly used maps are those in atlases. Useful atlas maps include important political and physical maps showing essential features of relief, climate and vegetation. When purchasing a set of atlases, you should consider the quality and level of detail of these maps, along with the provision of a good index using latitude and longitude. Look also at the quality and amount of other useful data sources within it, such as maps of communications, resources and indicators of development of various types.

It is also worth considering the use of an interactive online atlas if access to the Internet is a possibility for students. A particularly useful example can be found at:

- www.atlapedia.com

While the rote learning of the location of places is unlikely to be a common activity in Geography today, no geographer would suggest that a knowledge of the location of places is not of some value. It is through the regular use of atlases for skills development, rather than any contrived attempts at learning the maps, that locational features will be reinforced. These activities include:

- the calculation of distances and areas using different map scales;
- giving and following directions;
- the use of latitude and longitude to locate places which are listed in the index;
- recognising geographical characteristics from thematic maps (e.g. relief and climate) by using the map key and describing distributions of phenomena shown;
- using and interpreting different styles of map presentation (e.g. choropleth maps, dot distribution maps and topological maps);

- searching for relationships by comparing maps showing different types of information;
- using data such as climatic graphs and fact files.

A suggested approach to teaching atlas skills
The skills of using scale, direction and a map key are ones which you need to reinforce regularly. This exercise also incorporates the need to be able to use latitude and longitude references in the index. The competitive element introduces extra incentives to students.

The exercise works best in pairs, although it can be done individually, and you could use the idea as a stand-alone exercise with any atlas maps which show appropriate details. Alternatively, it could provide an introduction to a unit of work on a particular area (e.g. maps of Brazil could be used as an introduction to a study of a named developing country) or a particular theme (e.g. references to tourist destinations could be used to introduce that topic).

The following activity acts as part of an introduction to world contrasts.

Student activity 5.1

Working in pairs, students are asked to find a place they have not heard of on each of two maps of countries chosen from different continents. Using the key, scale and directions, they then create a multiple-choice question about each place they have found on the map. While students are often asked to answer questions, asking them to create questions is not frequently done. However, the creation of one correct alternative and three valid distractors ensures that great care is taken to use the appropriate skills and study the map information with care.

On completion, the questions are passed on to another pair for answering. Much valuable discussion and mutual studying of the map can take place if it is thought that an error has been made in setting a question. An extra dimension is the need to correctly use latitude and longitude to find the places initially, using the index. A competitive element is introduced if this is done as a timed activity.

The following are two examples of questions created by one pair of students. It becomes very clear that the successful creation of these questions is a valuable exercise in skills reinforcement.

1 Which of the following facts about Bialystok is not true?
   a) It is within 100 km of the coast.
   b) It is east of Bydgoszcz.

c) It is less than 200 metres above sea level.

   d) It is located on the railway line between Warsaw and Vilnius.

2 Which of the following statements about Chihuahua is true?

   a) It is on the eastern side of the Sierra Madre mountains.

   b) It is located on the Canchos River.

   c) It is north west of Culiacán.

   d) It is within 100 km of the international boundary between Mexico and the USA.

Using more detailed maps

The use of large scale maps (usually 1:25,000 or 1:50,000), showing small areas, is a valuable activity often incorporated into both teaching programmes and examination assessments. Frequently, teachers use maps which show the local area, although those showing parts of case study areas are also useful. It is through the regular use of such maps that physical and human features of areas can be identified and proficiency in specific mapwork skills practised by students. These include:

- the calculation of distances and areas using the scale;
- giving and following directions;
- using four- and six-figure grid references to locate places;
- recognising map symbols by using a key;
- recognising physical and human characteristics using map evidence;
- drawing and annotating cross-sections and sketch maps.

Regularly incorporating the study of detailed maps of areas into a series of work activities can be far more effective than carrying out mapwork tasks as discrete exercises. However, the availability of class sets of appropriate maps is often a problem. Mapwork opportunities are therefore often determined by the availability of sets of large scale maps which have been used in previous external examinations, or which are reproduced in textbooks.

It is, however, often possible to obtain detailed maps of your local area, either directly from the cartographer or through an appropriate supplier. One of the main producers of detailed maps (UK and international) is The Ordnance Survey, Romsey Road, Southampton, UK, SO16 4GU www.ordsvy.gov.uk. However, it is possible to obtain detailed maps of most locations from local suppliers.

The following examples are maps which have been used in previous IGCSE papers. For copyright reasons, CIE cannot sell any map extracts, but you may have sets available from a previous examination. If so, they could be used as part of thematic or case studies.

The Ulladale area of Zimbabwe shown in Figure 8 is a rural area from which minerals are extracted and there is map evidence of extractive industry and associated insfrastructural development. The area could be used as a case study of mineral extraction or it could be studied to illustrate the effects on people and the environment of extractive industry.

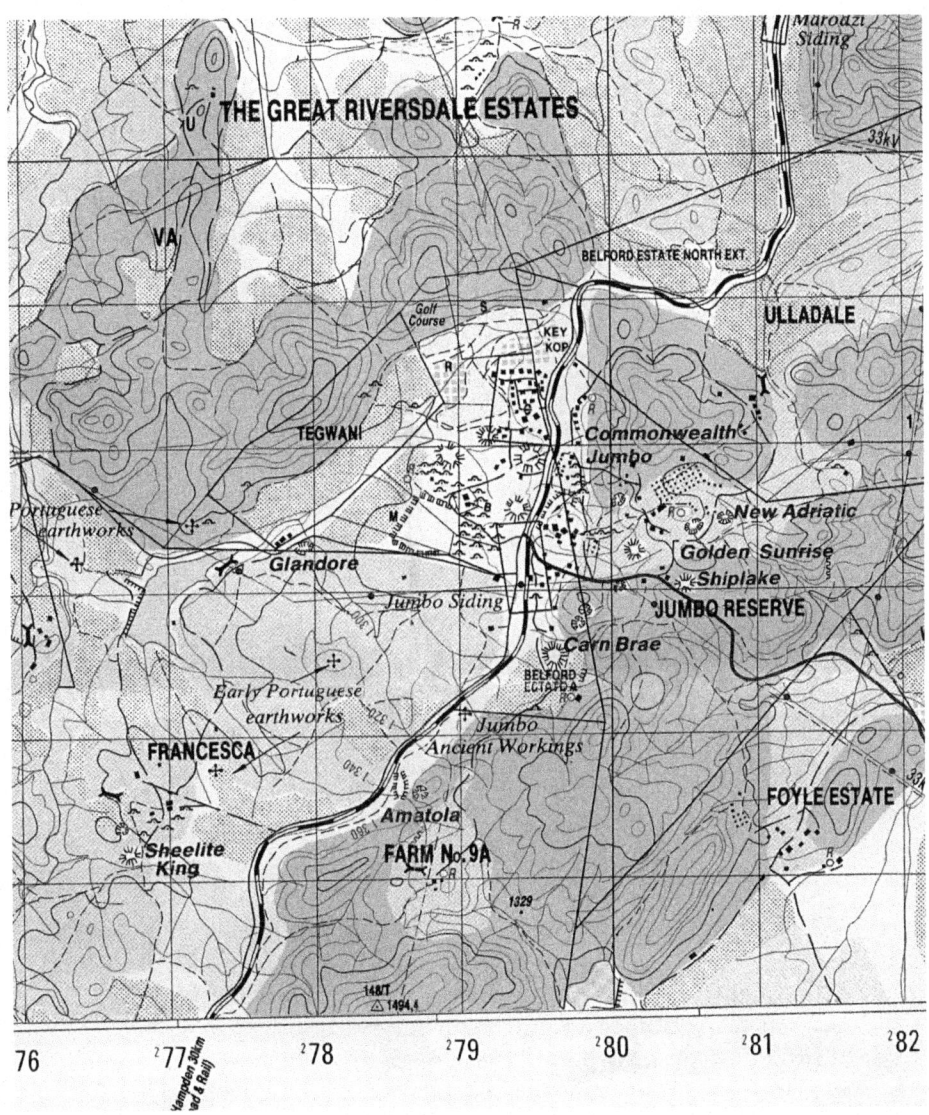

Figure 8: 1:50,000 Zimbabwe map extract © Government of Zimbabwe

The Mauritius map extract (Figure 9) shows the town of Bambous, which is a service provider for much of the surrounding area, a large proportion of which is used for sugar plantations. There is a factory which is used for processing the sugar cane at Medine. The area could be used for a case study of commercial agriculture or as part of a unit of work on the plantation system. Alternatively, it could be used as part of a unit of work on settlements and service provision.

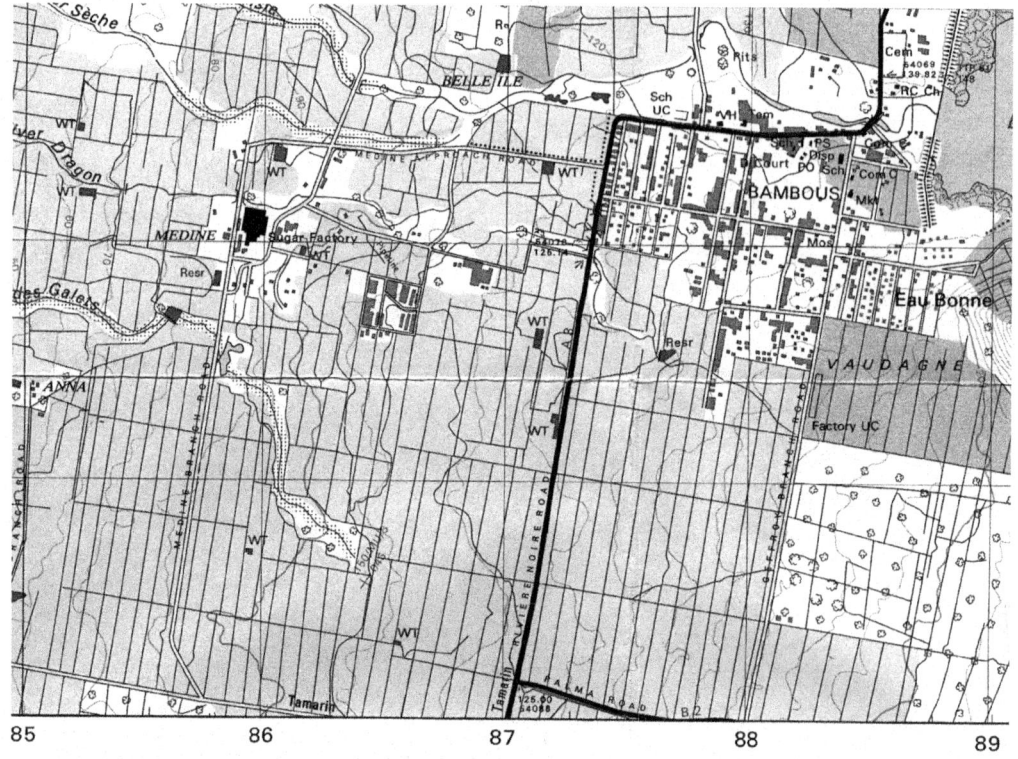

Figure 9: 1:25,000 Mauritius map extract © Government of Mauritius

Teacher activity 5.1

- What mapwork skills exercises could you devise using the map extracts from Zimbabwe and Mauritius?
- How could you incorporate these maps and skills exercises into your teaching programme?

If you do not have these maps available as class sets, you could carry out a similar exercise using any detailed map extract.

Use of photographs

Photographs are a very powerful tool that can be used to illustrate all aspects of Geography. They provide motivation and interest for students of all ages and abilities. Whatever is being studied, whether it is a series of physical processes and landforms or a human activity which dominates a landscape, it is likely that photographs will be available to bring it alive. Photographs of the aftermath of an event such as a natural disaster (e.g. an earthquake) or an environmental disaster (e.g. an oil tanker spillage) also present opportunities to involve students in empathising with people and the natural environment. As well as using them in the classroom for developing skills such as observation and interpretation, photographs can also be of value to students as part of their own research, with many using them to illustrate aspects of coursework enquiries.

Are you making the most of photographs in your lessons? Many textbooks are made to look attractive by the inclusion of photographic material, but if photographs are merely used as illustrations they are being underused. The following are examples of ways in which photographs can form the basis of activities which develop skills and understanding:

- developing observational skills and making deductions using evidence;
- producing annotated sketches of physical and human features from photographs;
- using aerial photographs and/or satellite images (along with maps of the area shown) to identify patterns and/or relationships between physical and human features;
- using photographic evidence to encourage an appreciation of the lifestyles of people in different parts of the world.

Suggested approaches to using photographs

Student activity 5.2

Figure 10 shows an everyday scene in Swaziland where a number of women are washing clothing in a stream close to their homes. As part of a scheme of work which contrasts the quality of life between countries at different levels of economic development, it provides opportunities for students to discuss in pairs or groups questions such as:

- What do you think the women are doing in the photograph?
- Is this a good way to do this everyday task?
  - How do you think the women feel who are shown in the picture?
  - How might the activities shown in the photograph affect the people who live in the area and the natural environment?

Figure 10: Washing in a stream, Swaziland

- What do you think the man is doing?
- What might the people be saying to each other?
- In what part of the world do you think the photograph was taken? On what evidence is this based?
- How does the activity shown compare with the way it is carried out in your own country?
- Why do the differences exist?
- In what other ways do you think the lives of the people shown will differ from those in your own country?

There is little doubt that students of all abilities will be able to respond well to questions such as these. They could make simple observations about aspects of quality of life along with raising more complex issues, such as the reasons for and impacts of lack of utilities such as piped water. In addition, if appropriate, the existence and significance of gender divisions can be raised.

Student activity 5.3

The aerial photograph in Figure 11 shows an expanding area of light industry on rural land at the edge of a large city in the United Kingdom. It offers much scope for skills development as part of a scheme of work

Figure 11: Light industry development – aerial view of Sherwood Park, United Kingdom

on the impacts of the changing location of industry. You could use photographs such as this for the following types of activity:

- Initial observations can be encouraged by the drawing and labelling of the main features (e.g. roads, edge of housing estate, woodland, grassland, new industrial buildings etc.). Depending on the skills and experience of students in this type of activity, it may be wise to provide an outline sketch and/or a list of features to identify and label.
- If available, it is worth using a detailed map of the area, along with the photograph, to identify features. Students enjoy relating the aerial view to a detailed map of the area and tasks can be set asking for particular features to be identified (e.g. if the industrial buildings are all identifiable on the map by name, three of them could be labelled A, B and C on the photograph to be named by students).
- Whether or not a map is also available, a detailed study of the photograph should be encouraged by focusing on significant aspects and asking questions which generate detailed description (e.g. of the buildings – size, building materials, style etc.).
- In order to link the aerial photograph with the issue being studied, you will need to generate tasks to direct students to the reasons for the growth and its effects on the rural environment. These could take

the form of questions for individuals, pairs or groups such as 'Why have these buildings been built here?' and 'What are the people in the nearby area of housing likely to think about the development?' Alternatively, students could take on roles, becoming involved in discussion in order to be able to understand the impacts of the development on the local people and environment.

- It is interesting to invite reasoned speculation as to what the area will be like in ten years' time. This could form an extension exercise.

Teacher activity 5.2

How do you make use of local maps and photographs in your school? It would be useful to find out what resources are available to use with your classes and carry out an audit of how these are used to help students build on geographical skills.

Try to obtain more maps of your local area, of different types and at different scales. You may, however, find that few detailed maps are available, either because they do not exist or because they are regarded as being of military value. Perhaps you may be able to obtain extra maps and/or aerial photographs by contacting the Surveyor General; alternatively, a local library may be a useful source of materials. You might be able to boost your supply of photographs of your local area if you have access to a digital camera.

Using current events as a stimulus to learning

There is little doubt that there are many advantages in using up-to-date resources. There are many topical, relevant and newsworthy events which can be used for geographical learning. While it is impossible to plan in advance for the inclusion of many local, national or global events of geographical significance in a teaching programme, there are others which, with a little forethought and imagination, you can include to enhance motivation.

It is sad that floods, drought, earthquakes, volcanic eruptions, hurricanes and other natural disasters seem to occur often. While it is not entirely predictable what disaster will occur, or where, it would be unusual if a recent or current example were not available to generate interest in Geography lessons. Always take the opportunity to collect and file away a collection of relevant news items, both from newspapers and on video, which are likely to be useful in forthcoming lessons. Significant news items will, of course, also be available on websites, both at the time of the event and for many months afterwards. These could be used as a source of information by you or your students. A useful website for finding articles from newspapers from all parts of the world is:

● www.onlinenewspapers.com

The extract on page 60 is just one example of an article which could be used. It was taken from the website of the Straits Times of Singapore in August 2002. The extract can be used in many ways in order to focus the attention of students on a relevant current event or issue. While it is possible simply to ask students to read and answer questions on the extract, there are more interesting ways in which such information can be used. For example, the places mentioned can be labelled on an outline map of the area and annotation added on the effects of the fires on people and the environment.

Suggested approaches to learning from sporting events

While natural disasters and many other currents events cannot directly be incorporated in planning, it is possible to plan to capitalise on interest generated amongst students by a major sporting event such as the football World Cup or the Olympic Games. Such international tournaments have universal appeal, with even people not usually interested in sport following the competition as the glamour and high profile personalities involved generate a vast amount of media attention.

Before the football World Cup in 2002, Japan and South Korea were just any other countries to many disaffected students. By the end of the tournament, many became much more interested in learning about the Geography of the host nations and were even able to locate Senegal on a world map after their defeat of the defending champions France in the opening match! There is much scope for harnessing this interest to practise geographical skills, gain spatial knowledge and introduce a number of geographical themes. You might like to try some of the following activities.

Student activity 5.4

Students can investigate the countries involved in the event. The information in the table on page 61 shows the huge contrasts between the 32 qualifying nations for the 2002 World Cup. The data could be mapped or graphed and further research could be carried out on the geographical characteristics of competing countries.

Flights cancelled in Malaysian Borneo as Sumatran 'hot spots' soar; slight haze in Singapore could continue for a week

Fires in Indonesia have begun to make their presence felt in neighbouring countries. In Malaysia, a thick haze has disrupted internal air services and forced flight cancellations in Malaysia's Sarawak state on Borneo island, an airport official said yesterday. Meanwhile, Singapore has been experiencing slightly hazy conditions over the last two days.

In a statement yesterday, the National Environment Agency said satellite pictures showed that the number of hot spots in Sumatra and Kalimantan had increased, and the prevailing south-westerly winds were carrying some of the smoke haze from southern Sumatra towards peninsular Malaysia and Singapore. In Malaysia, national carrier Malaysia Airlines has cancelled several flights by small aircraft since Thursday because of a deterioration in air quality, according to a spokesman for Sarawak's Miri Airport.

He said that a number of flights servicing the state's rural areas were either delayed or cancelled, as smaller planes which fly at lower altitudes could neither land nor take off in the hazy conditions. 'The air quality has become very bad and the low visibility makes flying the small planes very dangerous,' the spokesman said.

A spokesman for the Meteorological Department in Kuala Lumpur told AFP that visibility levels in Sarawak and neighbouring Sabah state on Friday were 'among the worst in years'. 'The visibility in those states is alarmingly low, and it could cause serious problems, aside from disrupting flight services,' the spokesman said.

'Everything has to be put on hold when the haze gets this bad, from agriculture to schooling, for health and security reasons.' The spokesman said it was too soon to tell if the haze would improve. But he added that little rain was expected in Sabah and Sarawak in the coming week. 'This is the dry season and every year it's the same thing,' he said. 'The burning in Sumatra and other parts of Indonesia causes us to be hit by the haze.'

In 1997 and 1998, choking haze caused by forest fires in Indonesia enveloped parts of South-east Asia for months. It caused serious health problems and traffic hazards, as well as disrupting airline schedules. The haze then caused an estimated US$9.3 billion (S$16.3 billion) in losses to regional economies.

Source: http://straitstimes.asia1.com.sg

Country	Continent	Total population (millions)	GNP (US$ per person per year	Urban population (%)
Argentina	South America	37.5	11,940	90
Brazil	South America	171.8	6,840	81
Ecuador	South America	12.9	2,820	62
Paraguay	South America	5.7	4,380	52
Uruguay	South America	3.4	8,750	92
Costa Rica	Central America	3.7	7,880	45
Mexico	Central America	99.6	8,070	74
USA	North America	284.5	31,910	75
Belgium	Europe	10.3	25,710	97
Croatia	Europe	4.7	7,260	54
Denmark	Europe	5.4	25,600	72
England	Europe	50.0	(UK)22,220	(UK) 90
France	Europe	59.2	23,020	74
Germany	Europe	82.2	23,510	86
Italy	Europe	57.8	22,000	90
Poland	Europe	38.6	8,390	62
Portugal	Europe	10.0	15,860	48
Republic of Ireland	Europe	3.8	22,460	58
Russia	Europe	144.4	6,990	73
Slovenia	Europe	2.0	16,050	50
Spain	Europe	39.8	17,850	64
Sweden	Europe	8.9	22,150	84
Turkey	Europe	66.3	6,440	66
Cameroon	Africa	15.8	1,490	48
Nigeria	Africa	26.6	770	36
Senegal	Africa	9.7	1,440	43
South Africa	Africa	43.6	8,710	54
Tunisia	Africa	9.7	5,700	62
China	Asia	1,273.3	3,550	62
Japan	Asia	127.1	25,170	78
Saudi Arabia	Asia	21.1	11,050	83
South Korea	Asia	48.8	15,530	79

Details about 2002 World Cup qualifiers. (Source: *Wideworld*, Vol.12, no. 4 April 2002)

Student activity 5.5

The theme of globalisation can be illustrated by using a major sporting event. The fact that countries are becoming much more interdependent through improved communications, trade and accessibility can be demonstrated by the Olympics or the World Cup. Clearly, globalisation does not necessarily bring equality, a fact that can be illustrated by reference to statistics which show that, for both competitions, the host cities have been heavily concentrated in more economically developed countries. For example, of 29 Olympic Games between 1896 and 2000 (including the cancelled ones of 1916, 1940 and 1944), 18 have been held in Europe and 6 in North America, with none at all in Africa and South America. The venues which can be found on the following website could be plotted on a world map and compared with population levels and indicators of development.

- www.internationalgames.net/olympic.htm

Student activity 5.6

The theme of inequality is also evident in Olympic medal performance. Statistics can easily be obtained to examine the correlation between the performance of athletes and economic development. This could be mapped using choropleth shading; alternatively, scatter graphs and/or statistical tests could be carried out using a variety of development indicators. Interpretation and discussion would then focus on why such inequalities exist. The medal table for the 2000 Sydney Olympics can be found at:

- www.olympics.smh.com.au/tally.html

Student activity 5.7

The theme of urban regeneration can be studied and exemplified by the use of materials relating to a major global sporting event. Both the short- and long-term impacts of the building of stadia and the economic significance of the event as part of the regeneration of an urban area and its infrastructure can form an interesting case study. This can incorporate issues of urban sustainability, which can be examined by looking at long-term impacts. For example, Barcelona (1992) is an excellent example of the Olympic Games triggering successful regeneration, its legacy including not only new sporting facilities but a new international airport terminal, a restructured rail network, a major investment in the road network and major urban environmental improvements.

Useful websites include:

- www.geog.plym.ac.uk/research/groups/olympic_games.htm
- www.gamesinfo.com.au
- www.panstadia.com/vol6/61-083.htm

Parents as resources

I have been asked many times by parents how they can provide help to their children to support their learning in Geography. The support and involvement of parents can make such a difference and it is all too easy to overlook the potential of parents as providers of resources, enthusiasm and motivation for students. The following ideas could be given to parents:

- Make sure that there are up-to-date atlases and road maps available in the house. Whenever possible, take the opportunity to encourage children to find places in the atlas or on the road maps. You could do this before going on holiday or if places are in the news. In addition, position a wall map or globe in your child's bedroom, or close to the television, and regularly use it to point out the location of places of significance.
- Encourage your child to read newspapers and geographical magazines or periodicals. Allow them to cut out interesting articles about places and stick them in a scrapbook, helping them to locate the places on the world map.
- Encourage your child to watch television programmes with geographical themes. There are many programmes of interest about the natural world and current events programmes often include articles of geographical significance. Discuss local and national news items with your child and encourage them to look up extra information on websites or in encyclopedias.
- There are several films on video or DVD of geographical interest (e.g. Dante's Peak, Medicine Man, Twister) which you could watch with your children, trying to generate discussion about geographical issues (e.g. Where is it taking place? Why is it happening? What will be the effects?).
- If you have access to the Internet, encourage your child to 'chat' to friends around the world using email. Alternatively, encourage them to write to pen pals in other countries. Try to guide them to find out about where their friends live, their lifestyle, the weather and other points of geographical interest.
- When travelling, talk to your child about landmarks and places you pass.
- Encourage them to follow the route on a road map. Try to point out features such as mountains, valleys and ports.

- Try to organise visits to a wide range of places of geographical interest (e.g. coastal resorts, capital city, nature reserves, areas of countryside). Get your child involved in planning the trip and collecting information about your destination. When there, show them interesting places, talk to them about the place you are visiting and help them to look at information boards and take photographs of what they see. If they want to stick these in a scrapbook, along with maps and a diary of their day, encourage this and always praise their efforts.
- Encourage them to become a member of a local, national or international environmental organisation (e.g. Worldwide Fund for Nature (WWF)) or a charitable organisation sponsoring development. You could suggest that a relative pays for one year's membership for a birthday or Christmas present. Find out about local environmental activities which take place during the school holidays.
- Sponsoring a child through an international organisation is a worthwhile and interesting activity which will generate much interest amongst the family about the Geography of the country in which the child who is being sponsored lives. The organisation will also provide information about the area and quality of life. Details can be obtained from organisations such as: www.plan-international.org

 LOOKING BACK

There is little doubt that the success or failure of many lessons depends on what resources are available for use. However, it is how these resources are used which is more important. Ask yourself the following questions:

- Are all the resources you use varied and stimulating?
- Do the resources you use match the needs of your students? If not, what could be done to make them more accessible to the least able and more stimulating for the most able?
- Are you using resources for skills development or simply as sources of information?
- Are all your resources up to date? If not, what strategies can be used to update your resource base?

6 Coursework and fieldwork activities

Fieldwork can be an enjoyable part of every Geography course. It may be the reason why many students choose to study Geography for examination courses and it can be one of the most rewarding aspects of a Geography teacher's job. The difficulties involved with the organisation and financing of fieldwork are usually outweighed by the benefits of experiential learning in an out-of-school setting. It facilitates the development of a wide range of skills which will have value well beyond their direct use in Geography.

This chapter briefly looks at syllabus requirements for coursework, using the CIE IGCSE Development Studies syllabus as an example, highlighting the advantages and disadvantages for both students and teachers of undertaking the coursework option of a syllabus. The role of the teacher in directing coursework is discussed, and how the teacher can use coursework to help develop generic skills. Finally, the alternatives to coursework – classroom-based enquiries and virtual reality field trips – are considered.

Wherever possible, you should include coursework as an integral part of your schemes of work. In some schools, fieldwork is still seen as the focus for occasional outings or a period of time in a residential field centre for a select group of students. However valuable this may be, it should be seen as a poor substitute for systematic and integrated activities built in to the scheme of work at regular intervals. If it is not possible to go further afield, you could still aim to fit it into the school timetable, carrying it out in and around the school.

The recognition of the value of fieldwork in Geography by awarding bodies has resulted in the integration of coursework into many syllabuses. The assessment objectives tested often include the collection, presentation and analysis of primary and secondary data of different types. This may be done through teacher-led coursework or individual investigations.

For example, the syllabus for CIE IGCSE Development Studies requires that the assessment objectives of investigation, participation and problem solving be tested by either a school-based coursework assignment, consisting of a project of a maximum of 5,000 words (Paper 3), or an 'Alternative to Coursework' examination (Paper 4), which is externally set and marked:

- Paper 3 requires the use of research techniques and a variety of sources in conducting an investigation into a development problem, proposing solutions and carrying out practical activities related to these solutions.
- Paper 4 provides candidates with a limited amount of data about a development problem which could provide the basis for a project. They are required to identify questions raised by the data and to indicate ways in which a project could be organised in order to identify and implement solutions.

Students who undertake coursework are expected to use different research techniques and a variety of sources in conducting an investigation, thus demonstrating their competence in the assessment objective of investigation. They should then show that they are able to analyse development problems and propose solutions, where appropriate carrying out practical activities in relation to the solutions. In this way, they will be able to fulfil the assessment objectives of participation and problem solving.

Advantages and disadvantages of coursework

The coursework option allows students to select their own topics for study, and can enhance enthusiasm and provide motivation. Carrying out an independent piece of investigative work helps build confidence and increase satisfaction. The advantages of coursework include the following:
- Assessment through a variety of methods benefits students who find examinations difficult. For those students, coursework is a valuable addition to the assessment process.
- Coursework is the best way of assessing the skills of investigation, participation and problem solving. It is harder to demonstrate these skills in an examination.
- Students often produce coursework of a high quality because they are highly motivated.
- Coursework enables students to see the relevance to the wider world of the subject which they are studying. It also enables the local environment to be used as a teaching resource.
- Coursework encourages independence, enabling students to organise their own work, while also offering the potential to develop cooperative skills.

Despite its many advantages, coursework does bring with it certain constraints and problems. These differ from those associated with externally set and marked examinations and should be taken into account when embarking on school-based assessment:
- Practical activities and fieldwork require careful planning and organisation and may impinge on time allocated to other subjects.

- The resources that are available, both financial and in terms of equipment and staffing, must be adequate to support the fieldwork activities.
- The skills of investigation need to be taught and practised over a long period of time. This should be done throughout the school, rather than the coursework being seen as an isolated exercise.
- Students who are completing coursework in several subjects may find that they have a heavy workload. It will be necessary to liaise with other teachers in terms of timing and deadlines.
- The length of time required to complete coursework tasks sometimes makes it difficult to keep some students interested, particularly the least able. Breaking the coursework down into clear sections, with interim deadlines, can be a helpful way of maintaining interest and providing feedback and encouragement.
- Careful supervision and guidance is necessary to make sure students apply the required skills and do not merely put their efforts into activities such as descriptive work, for little reward.
- Coursework may cause problems for students who change schools during the course.
- Work outside the classroom involves an element of risk and students will need to be made aware of appropriate safety and behavioural considerations, particularly if they are working unsupervised.

Teacher activity 6.1

Always remember that your personal safety is more important than the data which you are collecting

Never go into isolated places alone

Work in groups of three or more

If a person has an accident, one person should stay with them while another finds help

Be aware that in open countryside, particularly in the hills, low cloud or mist may descend quickly

Take warm and waterproof clothing with you

Take a supply of chocolate or other high energy food

Take a whistle and torch with you to make contact in an emergency

Always carry coins or a phone card

Respect the environment – don't drop litter

Figure 12: Warning leaflet on fieldwork safety

Figure 12 is an example of a warning leaflet given to students before embarking on fieldwork in a rural area. Do you think anything else should be added to reflect your local context?

It is equally important to be aware of risks when carrying out fieldwork in an urban area. Before carrying out urban fieldwork, design a leaflet to give out to students which identifies the main safety issues.

The sequence of enquiry

Whether coursework is teacher directed or carried out individually by students there are a number of clear stages which should be undertaken, as shown in Figure 13.

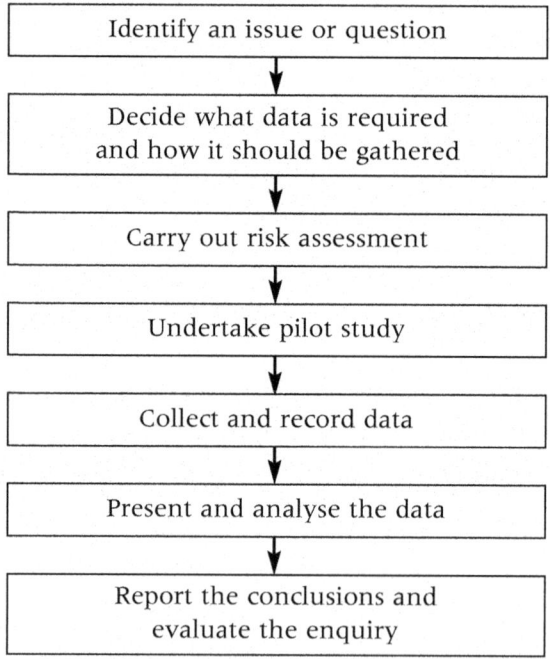

Figure 13: The sequence of enquiry for coursework

It is important to ensure that coursework tasks are differentiated so that all students will achieve their potential. Whatever their previous experience and training in investigative skills there will be few students who are able to follow the entire sequence individually. Many will need much guidance and teacher direction in order to follow an appropriate sequence of enquiry. Indeed, for some it will be necessary for you to

Assessment objective	0–4 Marks	5–8 Marks	9–12 Marks
Knowledge with understanding (within the context of teaching and guidance) (Max 12)	Describes information in simple geographical terms and shows a tentative grasp of the aims of the assignment within the geographical context of the course.	Provides adequate information using appropriate geographical terms and develops some associations between the aims of the assignment with relevant key ideas developed during the course.	Provides comprehensive information with a careful use of geographical terms and clearly links the aims of the assignment with relevant key ideas developed during the course.
Investigation (a) Observation and collection of data (Max 12)	Shows evidence of following basic guidance of the teacher on what to look for and how to record it, with some notion of planning.	Carefully applies basic guidance as explained in the planning of the various field exercises or collection of material. Personal initiative will also be evident.	Uses guidance to good effect and makes thorough observations and accurate recordings. Shows initiative in carrying out these tasks and may extend relevant information collected beyond the original design.
(b) Organisation and presentation (Max 12)	Methodology may be haphazard but uses at least one technique of representation effectively.	Sound methodology in which a range of techniques are applied competently and selectively.	Methodology logically pursued using a range of techniques appropriate to the line of enquiry. Individual flair apparent in a perceptive and coherent presentation.
Analysis (Max 12)	Makes descriptive statements and analysis is, therefore, limited. At least one statement attempts to analyse the data collected.	Makes a number of valid statements about the data collected and attempts to develop some explanations, including some in terms of cause and effect.	A thorough interpretation of the data with reasoned explanations and comments. Recognises weaknessess in the data if appropriate.
Judgement and decision making (evaluation and conclusions) (Max 12)	Superficial conclusions reveal limited judgements which are largely unsubstantiated. Links with original aims are tenuous.	Makes an attempt to relate to the original aims of the project in making some tentative conclusions. Some judgements are substantiated by the information collected.	Directly relates to the original aims in reaching conclusions. Makes a critical appraisal of assignment and may recognise its limitations and difficulties of reaching definite conclusions.

Note: 0 marks will be awarded if a candidate makes no attempt or an irrelevant attempt at an assignment, or part of an assignment, as assessed for the assessment objectives described above.

Source: CIE IGCSE Geography syllabus (2002)

identify the issue to be investigated and give very clear guidance on how and where data should be collected. You will need to give different amounts of assistance to students of varying abilities in the processes of data recording, presentation and analysis.

As can be seen from the example of an assessment matrix for CIE IGCSE Geography coursework on page 69, the degree of teacher direction should be reflected in the final outcome of the work, with those candidates who have been able to show autonomy and initiative being rewarded for their individual input. As in many syllabuses used by awarding bodies, levels of achievement are described for each of the five criteria being assessed.

It can clearly be seen that the highest level requires the need for considerable individual input at all stages of the enquiry sequence by the use of such phrases as 'shows initiative', 'may extend relevant information collected beyond the original design', and 'individual flair apparent'. In contrast, the lowest level recognises the need for considerable guidance for many students by the use of the phrase 'following basic teacher guidance'. While it is the provision of enough guidance which will enable less able candidates to be able to demonstrate their basic abilities, it is the provision of enough opportunities to demonstrate the ability to work independently, without teacher guidance, which will enable more able candidates to achieve their full potential.

A common approach which teachers use with many classes is to direct students to a particular theme or issue, with initial data collection exercises being largely teacher directed, and opportunities for individual input provided as extension exercises.

Suggested approaches to urban fieldwork

Urban fieldwork is popular in many schools as it offers plenty of scope for different types of fieldwork in an area which is relatively safe and often easy to get to, both for class visits and independent, individual fieldwork. Many begin such studies with a teacher-planned visit for all students, then offer the possibility for individuals to plan and carry out their own extension work.

Student activity 6.1

One suitable topic for study is service provision and it is possible to set up the basic question 'What are the characteristics of the Central Business District of Town X?' All students initially focus on this question by collecting data at specific locations, through the completion of data recording sheets, on the following three characteristics:

- ground floor land use;
- building heights;
- pedestrian flows.

Clearly, this activity is highly teacher directed and would enable all students access to an acceptable amount of relevant data to present and analyse with varying degrees of teacher support. Even the weakest, with plenty of support and direction at all stages, would be able to produce something of value and feel a sense of achievement. Some may need precise instructions on how to present the data. You may wish to provide them with outline maps to complete to show land use. You could specify graphs which can be used to show the data and provide writing frames to guide the analysis and conclusions.

However, those who are capable can easily be given the opportunity to work independently by offering opportunities to make their own decisions on choices of sample sites and methods of data presentation and analysis, providing extension activities where appropriate. Successful examples of data which could be collected on an individual basis and form the basis of successful extension activities include:

- Further relevant data obtained through observation within the CBD. For example, data on traffic flows and parking restrictions at various locations would be simple examples of ways for individuals to extend the database in a relevant way.
- The extension of the database by the use of questionnaires. Students could write and carry out questionnaires which determine for what purposes individuals use the CBD and how far its sphere of influence extends. This would be valid along with the original basic question, as it would enable a greater range of characteristics to be described and geographical terminology used. It would also offer the opportunity for students to display an understanding of the need for sampling and widen the opportunities for cartographic forms of data presentation and analysis.
- Similar data from the CBD of another town. This could be collected in the same way as that in the initial data collection exercise and the two CBDs compared. This would involve the student individually adjusting the enquiry question. 'How do the characteristics of the CBDs of Towns X and Y differ?' would be one possibility. However, 'To what extent do the CBDs of Towns X and Y fit with textbook theory?' would offer more possibilities to integrate theoretical work and display conceptual understanding.

- Comparative data collected from shopping centres in other parts of the same city, for example neighbourhood centres and out-of-town shopping centres. The focus of the enquiry could become a comparison of the different types of shopping centres with the question being altered accordingly.

The amount of initiative and individual input which could be shown by students in order to successfully extend their work in these and other similar ways, beyond the initial teacher-directed component, would enable them to demonstrate fully their capabilities in carrying out an investigation and achieve full marks.

Developing generic skills through Geography fieldwork

The wider role of Geography in the application of transferable skills has long been recognised and there are many opportunities which arise in a fieldwork context to develop transferable skills. These include communication skills, literacy and numeracy. Despite the fact that fieldwork is an essential element in many external examination syllabuses, Geography teachers often have to justify fieldwork to those colleagues who resent students being taken off site. Incorporating the development of such key skills into fieldwork programmes, and being prepared to provide evidence for their wider assessment, may help to raise the profile of Geography in the wider curriculum.

Example: developing numeracy through fieldwork

The gathering, manipulation and display of numerical data are important skills and opportunities to develop such competencies arise naturally as part of fieldwork exercises in Geography. Whether carrying out fieldwork in rural or urban areas, the gathering of data will inevitably involve the development of numeracy skills. Traffic and pedestrian counts are obvious examples, but most types of fieldwork will involve the use of numerical data in some way.

For example, Figures 14, 15 and 16 show students carrying out data collection which involves the measuring of physical landforms.

- In Figure 14, the ranging poles are being used to measure distances across the river's channel and the flow meter is being used to measure the velocity of the water. The students will need to calculate the speed of flow. They do this by observing the number of revolutions of the small impeller over a set period of time. From this number, it is necessary to skilfully manipulate the numerical data, then use a conversion graph.

Figure 14: Students carrying out fieldwork using ranging poles and flow meters

Figure 15: Students carrying out fieldwork using ranging poles and clinometers

Figure 16: Students carrying out fieldwork using quadrats

- Figure 15 shows a clinometer being used to measure and record the angle of slope of a valley side.
- Figure 16 shows students estimating percentage vegetation cover on grassland which has been affected by footpath erosion.

It is rare for the subsequent presentation and analysis of the data collected not to involve other skills involving manipulation and display of numbers. The students in Figure 14 may want to use their depth and width measurements to draw a cross-section of the channel. They may then test for the correlation between depth and speed of flow, by using a scatter graph or calculating a correlation coefficient. The students in Figure 15 will want to draw the valley profile by using a protractor to show the changing angles that they have measured. Having collected the data on percentage vegetation cover close to the footpath, the students in Figure 16 will need to consider how to display it using kite diagrams or located pie charts.

Classroom-based enquiries

In spite of the many and varied benefits of carrying out a systematic programme of fieldwork, there will be those centres where, for whatever reason, circumstances dictate that it may be neither practical nor desirable to complete a piece of coursework.

In such circumstances, an entry for an 'Alternative to coursework' examination may be the only possibility. There are, however, many ways in which the required skills associated with investigation can be developed, rather than depending on textbook or didactic preparation. There is certainly nothing to prevent students becoming familiar with the sequence of enquiry which would be implemented for a coursework investigation.

Within the classroom, an issue or question can be identified and data gathered. The main difference is that the bulk of the data is likely to be drawn from secondary data, resources available from published sources and statistical material from, for example, the Internet. This data can, nevertheless, be presented graphically and cartographically, then analysed, with conclusions ultimately being drawn. Exercises in research work involving planning, sampling, data collection, presentation and analysis can all be carried out in and around the classroom, using familiar topics.

A popular school-based example is to study the weather over a period of time, incorporating the use of weather instruments in school and external data sources from meteorological records. Studies of the sphere of influence of the school can be carried out, for example through school registers whereby the homes of students can be plotted on a map of the surroundings of the school, and data obtained from resources such as local newspapers and bus timetables; this gives practice in simple questionnaire design, mapping of results and analysis. Population movements can be studied in a limited way by interviewing parents, grandparents and other relatives. Such enquiries, undertaken largely within school, can be beneficial in many schools where circumstances prevent other fieldwork and coursework being carried out. When marking 'Alternative to coursework' examinations, the quality of answers always makes it clear which centres have prepared candidates by actually involving them in some sort of investigative work. This practical approach is to be recommended, as there is no real substitute for the experience of carrying out the type of tasks which such papers focus on.

Teacher activity 6.2

Topics which lend themselves to investigation in the classroom are those where information can be gathered from the school community. These include topics such as quality of life, aspects of population and settlement Geography, recreation and leisure and issues relating to the economic structure and employment.

For any of these topics, work out how students could devise and carry out effective research work within the classroom which would develop their investigative skills. You should consider how the initial stages, including group data collection, could be organised and how individual extension activities could be used in order for differentiation to be achieved.

Virtual reality field trips

As Geography is about people and places, learning about any location can be significantly enriched by visiting it. Often this is too difficult, and frequently distance makes it impossible, but the Internet can be used to 'visit' many different environments around the world and interact with them. While this type of activity should not be confused with carrying out an investigation by collecting primary or secondary data, it may be useful to incorporate it into programmes of study to enhance students' knowledge and understanding of places and themes. For example, look at http://astro.uchicago.edu/cara/vtour, which would fit into a unit of work being carried out on Antarctica. Do you think that this 'virtual field trip' would help your students appreciate the unique characteristics of an area which few people will ever have the opportunity to visit?

LOOKING BACK

Fieldwork makes Geography 'come alive' and, whether carried out locally or further afield, can be of immense benefit in skills development.

◆ Do you aim to incorporate fieldwork activities with all students?

◆ Would you like your students to carry out more fieldwork activities? If so, what practical difficulties are preventing you from building them into the curriculum? Is there any way in which these difficulties could be overcome?

◆ Does coursework seem to you to be an attractive alternative to an examination assessment? How could your students benefit more from it?

◆ To what extent do you think that fieldwork and coursework is a burden which creates extra work for you, or does its philosophy reflect what a good Geography teacher should be doing anyway?

7 Assessment in Geography

Formative and summative assessment

The purpose of **formative** assessment is to inform future teaching and learning by giving feedback to students and teachers. It encompasses many day-to-day assessment strategies which help us to make judgements about what students know, understand and can do. It also enables their strengths, weaknesses and misconceptions to be assessed, so that the next steps in their learning can be determined. Good practice is dependent on clear learning intentions being shared with students. Much formative assessment may be informal as teachers build up a profile of students' geographical capabilities through questioning and observing, along with regular marking of work of different types.

Summative assessment is carried out less frequently and it reviews learning. Some summative assessments are useful in the medium term, for example when they assess learning at the end of a unit of work. Others are more formal and act as the external assessments upon which external qualifications are based.

Thus a formative assessment can be seen to provide 'assessment *for* learning' while a summative assessment is an 'assessment *of* learning'. The link between them is that the formative assessment helps students to effectively follow a course of study in such a way as to lead to each one being able to achieve their full potential in the next summative assessment.

Assessment is effective only when the work of students is evaluated using clear criteria, which are consistently applied, and where the outcomes are used to direct future learning and curriculum planning. When devising schemes of work, you should not only be aware of the need to plan learning opportunities but also of the need to evaluate that learning. Ideally, assessment should:

- monitor the progress of each student by checking on the acquisition of knowledge, understanding and skills, thus enabling specific action to be taken as a result of diagnostic assessment;
- evaluate the effectiveness of teaching strategies so they can be adapted to achieve their objectives;

- discriminate between individuals within a group, discovering potential abilities and aptitudes and predicting future performance;
- be linked to reporting requirements, such that meaningful feedback is given to both students and their parents. It should convey its true meaning without discouraging those with low ability;
- make use of a variety of assessment opportunities, including self-assessment;
- reflect any national requirements or those of awarding bodies.

The following table shows how both formative and summative assessment strategies can be implemented in the short, medium and long term.

	Assessment strategies	Purpose of assessment
Short term (from week to week)	• Observation of work being carried out in class • Oral questioning • Regular marking of work assignments • Written self-assessment by students	**Formative** • To inform interventions and planning • To give feedback to students so they can set short-term targets • To correct errors or misconceptions • To monitor short-term progress
Medium term (over a term or on completion of a topic)	• End-of-unit assessment tasks • End-of-term progress tests • Assessment of geographical enquiries • Written self-assessment by students	**Formative/summative** • To give feedback to students and agree criterion-related targets for improvement • To monitor and judge progress
Long term (over a year or at the end of a course of study)	• End-of-year examinations • Assessment of portfolio of a variety of work assignments against criteria • Assessment of completed coursework or individual study • Attainment summary using professional judgement • External examination	**Summative** • To inform next year's teacher • To inform parents • To evaluate, monitor and exemplify standards and attainment • To select and monitor departmental targets for improvement • To obtain recognised qualification

Complete a grid based on the outline below which lists all the formative and summative assessments which you are using with each of your classes.

Is your assessment fair and effective? Do you use a variety of strategies?

Description of assessment	Skills, understanding and areas of knowledge tested	Formative or summative?	End of year	Periodic	Contin-uous

Examples of effective formative assessment

Review of previous learning through oral questioning

Many lessons start with a quick review of work previously covered by using a short question-and-answer session. Thus, following a lesson which introduces the main flows and stores within the drainage basin, you would need to make sure that these processes are understood in order to ensure that a firm foundation has been laid. Without ensuring, and if necessary reinforcing, the understanding of the processes of groundwater flow, and the more rapid channel flow and overland flow, there would be little point in introducing students to storm hydrographs and expecting them to be able to use them to explain the concept of lag time.

Sharing learning objectives

In order to work effectively, students need to be fully informed about what they are expected to learn and do. If you establish clear objectives and share them with your students, they will be better able to understand what is required of them and assess for themselves whether these objectives have been achieved. For example, as part of a unit of work on industrialisation a case study of Taiwan could be carried out. You could tell them:

We are going to use Taiwan as an example of a country where economic growth has been rapid. You will be looking at graphs to show changes in the economy of the country and you will need to work out what these show. You will need to learn how and understand why the economy has grown in the last 50 years.

You will notice that objectives in terms of knowledge, understanding and skills are all identified. At the end of the case study, students could either be asked orally whether these have been achieved or be asked to fill in a simple self-assessment.

Written comments on work of students

These are a vital part of formative assessment and should offer feedback to students in the form of a description of the strengths and weaknesses of their work, together with suggestions for future improvement. Whether the work being assessed is in the form of written work or oral work, in exercise books or on a wall display, or based on common class tasks or investigation, it can still be assessed effectively in this way. Similarly, whether testing skills, understanding or knowledge, written formative assessment can provide useful feedback for students.

In terms of formative assessment strategies there is little value in simply providing students with marks out of ten or letter grades reflecting effort and/or achievement. On completion of the case study of Taiwan used in the previous example, the following types of written comment may be pertinent:

It was a good idea to include a map but it would have been useful for you to fully label it to show the location of Taiwan.

You have identified the changes shown by the graph correctly. It would also help if you quoted figures to back up your statements.

Your explanation of why new industries grew up in Taiwan is excellent. This amount of detail will be very helpful in your revision.

Note that in each case an attempt has been made to be positive and offer encouragement for praiseworthy endeavour. Specific suggestions are also given for improvement. Comments such as 'good work' and 'well done' are of little intrinsic value.

Self-assessment by students

This strategy provides students with an opportunity to reflect on their own standards and set targets for improvement. Allied to your written comments, it can be a useful tool. Thus, following an investigation, students might be asked to complete a form such as the one on page 81.

Name .... **Form** .... **Date** ....

Title of investigation ....

What methods did you use to collect your information? ....

....

How successful were each of these methods? ....

....

Is there anything else you could have done to collect information?

....

What methods did you use to present your data? ....

....

Were there any other methods which you could have used? ....

....

Are you pleased with your written analysis? ....

....

What were your main conclusions? ....

....

Did you understand all your teacher's instructions? If not, what did you
find hard to understand?

....

Did you understand your teacher's comments? ....

....

What would you do to improve your skills in geographical investigations
next time you are asked to complete one?

....

Signature of student .... **Signature of teacher** ....

It is useful for you to look at these self-assessments and talk them over with your students before filing them. Before the next geographical investigation, it would be useful to let students remind themselves of their previous comments.

Improving examination performance

Despite the many and varied advantages to students of following a course in Geography, there is little doubt that the most frequent way in which your success as a teacher will be judged will be as a result of the scrutiny of the external examination results of your students. By definition, an examination will grade students according to their competence. However, the examination results of a group of students will generally reflect the quality of teaching and learning throughout the course. While no one would expect high grades from all students, there are strategies which can be used prior to the examinations which are likely to boost the performance of many candidates. The use of carefully planned revision strategies for your classes, along with the regular practice of examination questions, will enable you to give students the advice they need to achieve their maximum potential.

Class and individual revision strategies

You should plan to finish teaching the course well before the date of any external examination to allow time for a programme of class revision activities. Much of the knowledge and understanding required, including case studies, will be learnt individually. Nevertheless, activities in class can be structured around revisiting the topics studied and carrying out activities where all students are involved, rather than expecting them to be revising in silence or continually answering past questions.

Here are a few different activities which can be used successfully to keep students interested. The list is by no means exhaustive; it merely shows how revision activities need not be boring.

Student activity 7.1

This activity revisits topics, checking that key words and definitions are known. For each topic, a list of key words could be given out and matched with a series of definitions. You could do this as a card-sorting exercise. Alternatively, try making the exercise into a game. All of the group are given a blank playing card, which consists of six squares. The teacher produces a list of key words which need to be learnt for that topic, from which students are each asked to insert six in the squares on their grid. You should then call out clues at random, which consist of the definitions of the key words. Students cross out each word on their card as they recognise it from the definitions and the winner is the first to cross out all the words.

When revising many topics, it is necessary to learn lists. Why not try challenging students to produce acronyms to help them to learn lists? For example, the 'push' factors which encourage people to migrate from rural areas in developing countries are:

Soil erosion
Insufficient health care
Drought
Overgrazing
Famine
Reform of land
Unemployment
Mechanisation

Remember 'Sid of Rum'. The activity is enjoyable, revises the topic and each mnemonic invented may be a helpful revision aid.

Much of the information which has been recorded during the course will be in written form, so why not challenge students to work in groups to transfer some of this to presentations in the form of annotated sketch maps or diagrams which summarise the main points? This could be done on a wall display or perhaps an overhead transparency. Alternatively, challenge groups to produce PowerPoint presentations on a series of case studies. The presentations can be assessed by the class using a scoring system. This should incorporate a mark for content and use of terminology, as well as a mark for 'professional' appearance.

Case studies need to be learned and matched to question requirements. Each student could produce a world map where case studies are located, colour coded to match the appropriate section of the syllabus, and/or matched with context (e.g. LEDC or MEDC) by the symbol used. A list of case studies required by questions on past papers can then be given out and examples from the map matched with it.

Structure of examination questions

As part of examination preparation, it is essential that students become familiar with the style and structure of questions set in previous years. They should also have a confident grasp of the command words used by examiners. It is vital that they are aware of the type of mark schemes which are used, and how marks can be gained and lost. Periodically, they should prepare for, and answer, a series of carefully selected past questions on the topics being revised, with individual and class feedback being given to improve performance.

Students will need to be given plenty of advice and practice in responding correctly to **command words**. You should help them to build up a glossary of command words which identify what students need to do in their answers. These can be divided into seven broad categories.

1 Recall a piece of information, example or fact

identify state name give

These are command words which indicate that a concise brief answer is required.

For example:

- **Identify** the type of bridge used to cross the River Murowodzi at 830835.
- **State** the evidence which suggests that minerals are extracted in the area between grid lines 66 and 69.
- **Name** the city which has experienced counter urbanisation between 1990 and 2000.
- **Give** an example of a coastal feature formed by depositional processes.

2 Give a definition

define what is meant by give the meaning of

These command words indicate that knowledge is to be shown on the meaning of geographical terminology.

For example:

- **Define** the term 'primary sector'.
- **What is meant by** 'life expectancy'?
- **Give the meaning of** the term 'sustainable development'.

3 Provide a description

describe

This is a commonly used command word which invites candidates to write about the features of a particular feature or location. The amount of detail required is indicated by the mark allocation.

For example:

- **Describe** the annual distribution of rainfall in graph D. (1)
  (Here only one point would be expected, for example that there is more rain in the summer months.)

- **Describe** the physical features of the Umzingwani River, between its confluence with the Inyankuni river and the southern edge of the map. (4)

  (Here the mark allocation suggest that four pieces of map evidence are required.)

4 Give an explanation

explain   give/suggest reasons for   why

These command words are commonly testing understanding, for example of the formation of physical features or human patterns.

For example:

- **Explain** how a coral reef is formed.
- **Suggest reasons** why the area shown in the photograph is sparsely populated.
- **Why** do many people in developing countries still have large families?

5 Identify differences

compare   contrast   identify the differences between

These command words require two items to be considered and relevant differences and/or similarities identified. It may be acceptable to write two separate sentences or paragraphs describing each item. However, it is better to compare by using words such as 'whereas'.

For example:

- **Compare** the main features of commercial and subsistence farming.
- **Contrast** the location of the deciduous woodlands and coniferous forests shown on the map.
- **Identify the differences between** the employment structures of countries X and Y.

6 Make a judgement

evaluate   to what extent

These command words require a judgement to be made or an opinion to be expressed. The question may also ask for evidence to support it. The use of the term 'to what extent' suggests that there is not a perfect relationship between the two phenomena and a high level answer may well be able to recognise this.

For example:

- **Evaluate** the success of methods which have been used to reduce population growth rates in China.
- **To what extent** has government legislation reduced problems caused by atmospheric pollution?

(In this case, the high level answer would recognise that the legislation has had positive effects yet acknowledge that atmospheric pollution may still not have been entirely eliminated in spite of the legislation.)

7 Use a case study

> refer to an area which you have studied   by using an example
> for a named

Here a case study is required and care should be taken to choose one in the correct context.

- What are the benefits and disadvantages of the tourist industry to local residents? You should **refer to an area which you have studied** in an LEDC.
- **By using an example** which you have studied explain the causes of international migration.
- **For a named** urban area in Singapore, describe the attempts which have been made to improve quality of life.

Teacher activity 7.2

Using Figure 17 as stimulus material, write questions which use different command words which could be used by students to practice answering questions which require them to:
- recall a piece of information, example or fact;
- give a definition;
- provide a description;
- give an explanation;
- identify differences;
- make a judgement.

Figure 17: Transport in central Prague

Mark schemes

In order to give students appropriate advice on writing answers to examination questions which require more detailed responses, it is important that you become familiar with, and share with students, the mark schemes which are used by external awarding bodies. Copies of the 'Reports to Centres', which are written by Principal Examiners, along with published copies of mark schemes can prove extremely useful.

The two main types of mark scheme used in Geography examinations are point mark schemes and levels of response mark schemes. Point mark schemes are very familiar and will give credit for each relevant point made. They normally use the principle of one mark being awarded for each appropriate point made. Further marks may be awarded for using geographical terminology or developing or exemplifying ideas more fully. If a question has more than one component within it, there may be a number of marks reserved for each component, along with a mark for naming an example if this is required.

Level of response mark schemes, while used in some Geography examinations, are less familiar. Rather than accumulating marks entirely on the basis of the quantity of material written, a level of response mark scheme will differentiate between the quality of the answer, which could be measured in a variety of ways (e.g. they provide scope for rewarding short but high order answers which show perception or a high degree of abstraction).

Level of response mark schemes are most appropriate to questions which:
- require an answer in extended prose, either description or explanation;
- are open ended, as differentiation is by outcome;
- assess understanding, rather than simple recall of knowledge;
- involve expressing views, making judgements and supporting them with evidence;
- use command words which may trigger answers of varying degrees of complexity (e.g. explain, justify, suggest), and thus generate answers which show different levels of conceptual understanding;
- could be answered in different but equally acceptable ways;
- have sufficient marks to allocate at least two marks per level;
- require a balanced answer in higher level responses.

Their advantages include:
- enabling the 'quality' of answers to be assessed;
- providing scope for rewarding short but high order answers which, for example, show perception or a high degree of abstraction;
- allowing imaginative responses to be credited fully;
- offering scope to consider breadth of answers, where a greater number of points of the same quality could gain higher reward.

They are likely to incorporate a series of clear steps (or hurdles) between levels. Note how, in the mark scheme to the following example, an increase in quality of response is required as levels and therefore marks increase.

Example 1: Describe and suggest reasons for the differences in levels of nitrates along the course of the River Leen shown in Figure 18.

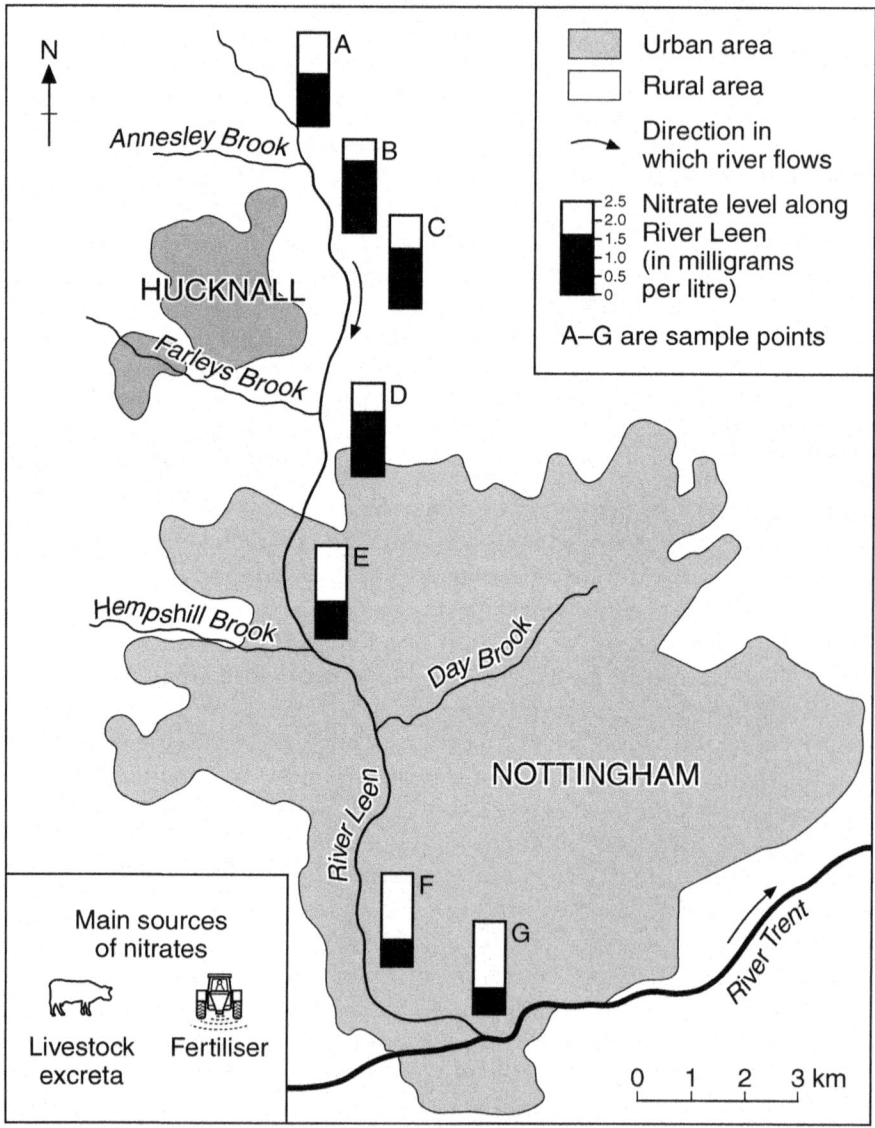

Figure 18: Map of River Leen, United Kingdom (Source: OCR)

Level	Type of answer	Example
1	Descriptive statements	Levels of nitrates are lower in the southern part, close to the River Trent.
2	Simple explanations (no elaboration)	Levels of nitrates are lower in the southern part as it is flowing through an urban area rather than a rural area which it flows through in the north.
3	Elaborated explanations	Levels of nitrates are higher in the northern part where it flows through a more rural area where livestock excreta and fertiliser pollute it.
4	Linked explanations	Levels decrease downstream as when it flows through the urban area the pollutants from livestock and fertiliser from rural areas upstream have been diluted by water entering from tributaries.

The following example shows how levels marking can be used for case studies, thus enabling greater reward for case studies showing place-specific detail compared with those that simply provide generic information with the name of a place added.

Example 2: Describe the effects of an earthquake in a named area on people and the local economy.

Level	Type of answer	Example
1	Statements including limited detail to describe the effects	People killed, buildings destroyed, roads destroyed, fires, injuries
2	More developed statements which describe the effects	Number killed, type of building destroyed, bridges collapse, electricity cables snapped, cost of damage, homelessness
3	Use of named example – comprehensive, accurate and place-specific statements	Los Angeles: Santa Monica freeway bridge collapsed, cost of damage to properties in the San Fernando Valley estimated at $20 billion

Make sure you find out which type of mark schemes are used by the awarding body which sets and marks the papers for your students. Show your students how the mark schemes work and give them practice in writing answers to try to achieve the highest levels. If you set a mock examination, this will provide you with an ideal opportunity to raise awareness among your students of the best strategies to use in writing answers. It is also a good time for a self-assessment to be completed, with students producing action plans to improve future examination performance (e.g. learn the meanings of all command words, have a more secure knowledge of case studies, improve examination time management etc.). You could then match student needs with individual and group revision strategies.

Advice for students about to take their external examinations

As the examination system is perpetual, experienced examiners and teachers will be able to identify familiar errors which result in underachievement. However, you must remember that, each year, the examination is a unique experience for that particular group of students. Consequently, it would be useful to share the following advice with candidates about to embark on their final preparation. You could give them the information in a handout, but it would be far better to talk through each point, using examples to illustrate it.

- Make sure you know the examination rubric. Read and obey the instructions on the front cover. Do not answer all questions if you are asked to make a choice.
- Ensure that the correct equipment is brought to the examination including pen, pencil, ruler, rubber and calculator.
- Read each question carefully, paying particular attention to command words (e.g. do not explain when only a description is asked for). Underline (or highlight in some other way) the key words in each question.
- Be careful when making your choice of case study. If the question asks you to choose an example from an LEDC, do not choose one from an MEDC. If the question asks you to choose a country, do not choose a city or continent. Learn the details of case studies, particularly those which are place specific, to give them authenticity.
- Be aware that questions are usually based around a theme which will provide a link between sections. However, be prepared to recognise any change of emphasis within the question focus.
- Do not repeat the same answer in different sections – such answers do not usually gain double credit.
- Use all the resources and do not ignore resources such as maps, photographs and diagrams which are provided. Be precise when using information from maps, graphs and diagrams and make sure you include the correct units when asked for measurements.

- Use the number of marks available for a question as a guide to the number of points needed. Do not write a full page of information if the question is only worth two marks. However, be prepared to develop ideas and extend answers in order to increase the marks which can be awarded in questions which are worth a larger number of marks.
- If level of response marking is used, make sure you know what the requirements are of the top level of response and structure your answers to achieve this.
- Be aware of how much time you are taking to answer each section of the examination paper and use your time wisely. Do not spend half the examination time on answering the first question and have to rush through the remaining three questions. Do not sit back when you have completed your answers. Read your answers again and check them, adding more facts and ideas if you can remember them.

 LOOKING BACK

Assessment of work carried out by students needs to be carefully planned. The guidance provided by the use of formative assessment will always prove to be of benefit and enhance individual achievement. With great emphasis being placed on the results of external assessments, time should always be allowed for planned preparation and revision activities.

- How effective are your methods of formative assessment, particularly your marking strategies? Should you be including more advice to your students and setting targets for future improvement, rather than simply reporting on their achievements or efforts?
- Do you give your students regular opportunities to carry out self-assessment? If not, what practical difficulties are preventing you from building them into your programmes of study? Are there ways in which these difficulties could be overcome?
- Do you aim to complete programmes of study in good time to incorporate planned revision activities with all students? Think carefully about how you can build in advice on command words and share information about marking schemes which will help students to target their answers in an effective way.

Appendix A: sources of information

Useful websites

To provide an exhaustive list of useful websites is impossible. Each time I look, I find something new. To aid searches for particular topics, there are many good search engines. I find Google a particularly useful one:

- www.google.com

The following list gives a flavour of the type of material which I have found on the Internet and used either with students or for personal research.

Sites with links to other geography websites

- www.colorado.edu/geography/virtdept/resources/startplc/start.htm
- http://geography.pinetree.org/
- http://members.aol.com/bowermanb/101.html
- www.georesources.co.uk
- www.geographyportal.co.uk
- www.zephryus.demon.co.uk/geography/topics.html
- www.pavilion.co.uk/dwakefield

Environmental geography websites

- www.greenpeace.org
- www.foe.org
- www.wwflearning.co.uk
- www.ourplanet.com/imgversn/planethme.html
- www.ddluk.com/oilspill (environmental effects of an oil spill)
- www.schools.detr.gov.uk/global/index.htm (global warming)
- www.teatrail.co.uk (ecology as it pertains to the world of tea)
- http://darwin.bio.uci.edu/~sustain/bio65/Titlpage.htm (biodiversity)
- http://conbio.net/vl/ (endangered species, international treaties, and biodiversity)
- http://endangered.fws.gov (endangered plants and animals)
- www.ran.org/ kids_action (rainforest)
- http://eduweb.com/amazon.html (Amazon rainforest)

Websites on earthquakes and volcanoes

- http://quake.seismo.unr.edu/ftp/pub/louie/class/100/seismic-waves.html
- http://quake.seismo.unr.edu/ftp/pub/louie/class/100/plate-tectonics.html
- http://volcano.und.nodak.edu

Weather and climate websites

- www.met-office.gov.uk/education/index
- www.4seasons.org.uk
- www.tornadoproject.com

Websites providing global statistics

- www.geohive.com/
- www.infoplease.com/ipa/A0004372.html
- www.odci.gov/cia/publications/factbook

Online atlases and statistics

- www.atlapedia.com
- www.sitesatlas.com

Physical geography website

- www.geog.ouc.bc.ca/physgeog

Searchable glossary providing concise definitions of key terms

- http://geography.about.com/library/misc/blgg.htm?terms=glossary

Links to virtual fieldwork websites

- www.georesources.co.uk/indexvf.htm

Website providing online answers to homework questions with a searchable database of answers to previous questions

- www.4learning.co.uk/apps/homework/index.jsp

Useful references

These are printed sources to which I have referred in the writing of this book. Again, while I am not suggesting that they are the only useful references for advice on teaching geography, they do contain much useful information.

Carter, R. (ed.) (1999) *Leading geography*, Geographical Association

Chalkley, B. and Essex, S. (2000) 'Learning from the Olympic Games', *Teaching Geography*, July 2000, 112–18

Corney, G. (2001) 'What is Geography', *Geography Review*, 15(2), 1

Feerick-Dornan, M. (1999) 'Home and away', *Teaching Geography*, January 1999, 40–1

Flinders, K. (2001) *A new introduction to geography for OCR GCSE Specification A*, Hodder and Stoughton

Foskett, N. (2000) 'Fieldwork and the development of thinking skills', *Teaching Geography*, July 2000, 126–9

Geographical Association (1999) *Geography in the curriculum*

Hassell, D. and Warner, H. (1995) *Using IT to enhance geography*, Geographical Association and National Council for Educational Technology

Hopkin, J. (2000) 'Assessment for learning in Geography', *Teaching Geography*, January 2000, 42–4

Howes, N. and Hopkin, J. (2000) 'Improving formative assessment in Geography', *Teaching Geography*, July 2000, 147–9

Leat, D. (1997) *Thinking through Geography*, Chris Kington Publishing

Leat, D. and McGrane, J. (2000) 'Diagnostic and formative assessment of students' thinking', *Teaching Geography*, January 2000, 4–7

Nowicki, M. (1999) 'Developing key skills through geography fieldwork', *Teaching Geography*, July 1999, 116–21

Worldaware (writing for the Department for International Development (DFID)) (2001) *Global Eye*, 16, Autumn 2001

There also are many useful references on the Standards site of the UK Department for Education and Skills at:

- www.standards.dfes.gov.uk

In the UK, many useful publications and periodicals can be obtained from the Geographical Association:
160 Solly Street
Sheffield
S1 4BF
UK
Email: ga@geography.org.uk

You may find that there is an organisation promoting geography in your country. There are two examples below for teachers in Australia and Singapore:
Dr Glenn Banks
Secretary, IAG
Department of Geography and Oceanography
Australian Defence Force Academy
Canberra ACT 2600, Australia
Email: g.banks@adfa.edu.aunks

The Geography Teachers' Association of Singapore
PO Box 212
22 Sixth Avenue
Singapore 276480
Website: http://homepage.mac.com/voyager/gta

Appendix B: glossary

Here is a list of important words or terms used in this book with which you should be familiar.

Active learning	using teaching styles which involve students participating fully in learning activities
Aims	the educational purposes of a course of study
Assessment	the making of informal or formal judgement to assess abilities, achievement and progress
Assessment objectives	interrelated or independent sets of skills and activities which are assessed and enable students to demonstrate achievement
Assessment structure	the methods which will be used to assess what candidates know, understand and can do
Auditory learning	learning by hearing
Awarding body	an organisation which will externally assess and certificate the work of students
Command word	a word used in an examination question which provides instruction to candidates
Coursework	work carried out by students, often as part of an external qualification, which is assessed by the teacher and moderated by the awarding body
Curriculum planning	the preparation of courses of study for students, including skills opportunities, teaching content and assessment opportunities
Diagnostic assessment	methods of consideration of abilities of students in order to establish strengths and weaknesses
Didactic approach	a form of learning based on formal exposition from the teacher
Differentiation	a planned process of intervention in the classroom to maximise potential based on individual needs
Evaluation	assessment of the success of a methodology or piece of work
Fieldwork	the collection of geographical information and data outside the classroom

Formative assessment	assessment which is designed to inform future teaching and learning by giving feedback to students and teachers
Generic skills	transferable abilities, such as numeracy and literacy, which students will use in other subjects as well as Geography
Geographical information system (GIS)	a computer system which is capable of assembling, storing, manipulating and displaying geographically referenced inform-ation (i.e. data identified according to location)
Information and communications technology (ICT)	media such as computers, including the internet, TV and radio
Kinaesthetic learning	learning by doing
Level of response marking	a method of marking examination answers which judges their quality, not necessarily their length
Mixed ability teaching	working with groups of students within a class with a wide variety of abilities
Point marking	a method of marking examination answers which judges the amount of relevant points made and rewards on the basis of one mark per point or idea
Self-assessment	judgement made by students on their own progress, often by the completion of forms
Sequence of enquiry	stages which should be undertaken in the completion of a geographical investigation
Setting	placing students in teaching groups with others judged to possess similar ability in the subject
Summative assessment	assessment which reviews learning at the end of a unit or course of study, often as part of a formal qualifications award
Teacher guidance	providing support for students, for example in lessons and when carrying out coursework assessments, in order that they achieve their full potential
Teaching strategy	a method devised to facilitate learning
Visual learning	learning by seeing

Index

Other titles in the Professional Development for Teachers series

Lightning Source UK Ltd.
Milton Keynes UK
UKOW04f1834220817
307772UK00001B/68/P